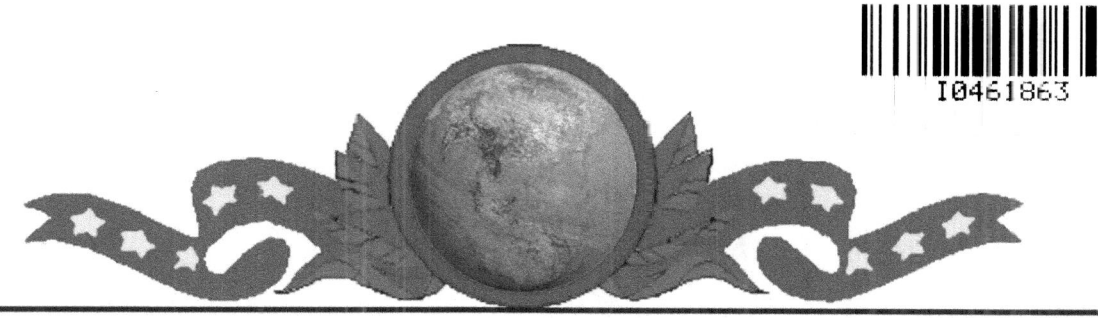

Real World
Colouring Book
For Advanced Users & Adults

Copyright 2019 By John Boom

50 Images

Created From Real Life Photos
For You To Colour As You Please.

I0461863

ISBN 978-0-359-82511-0
90000

9 780359 825110

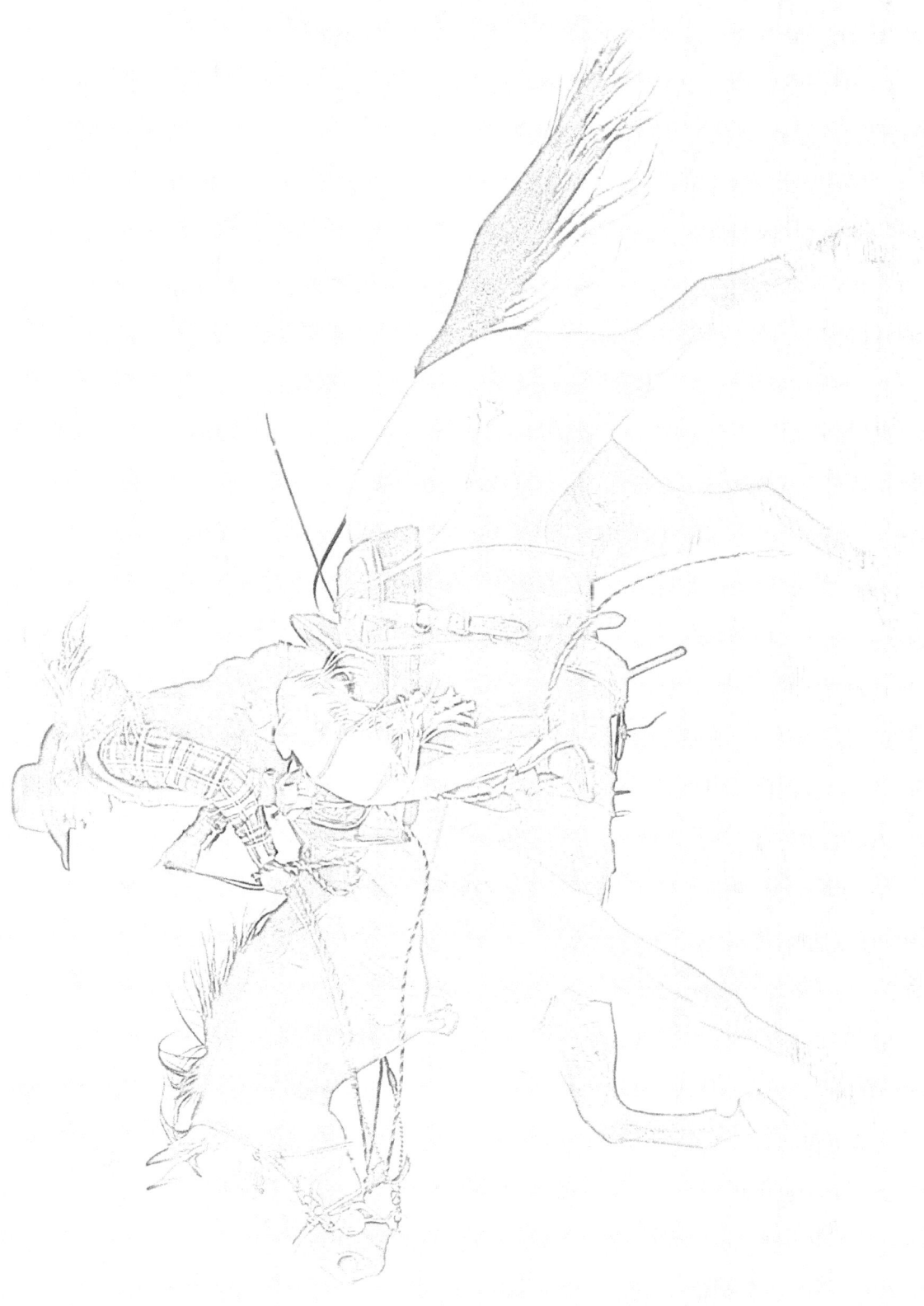

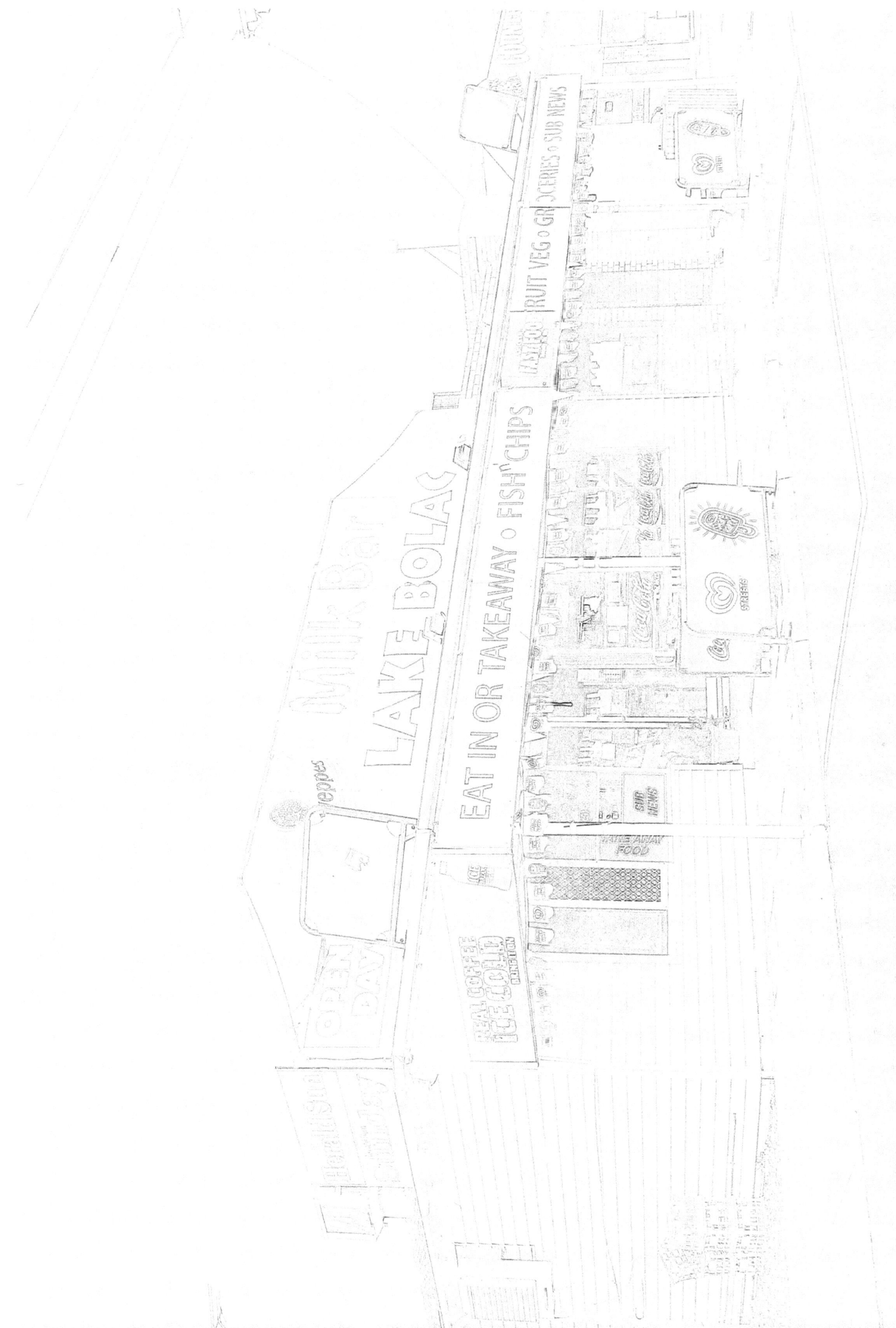

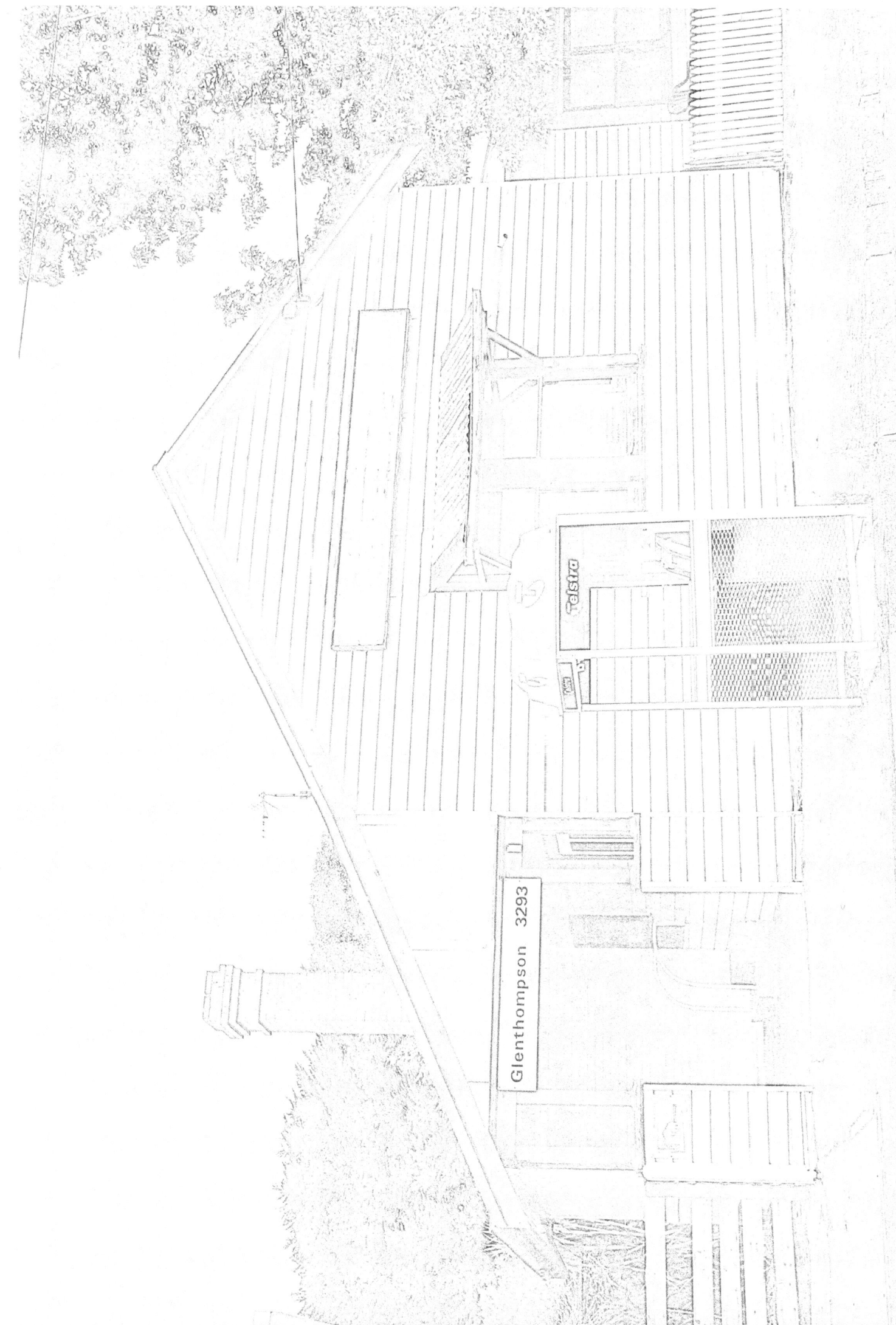

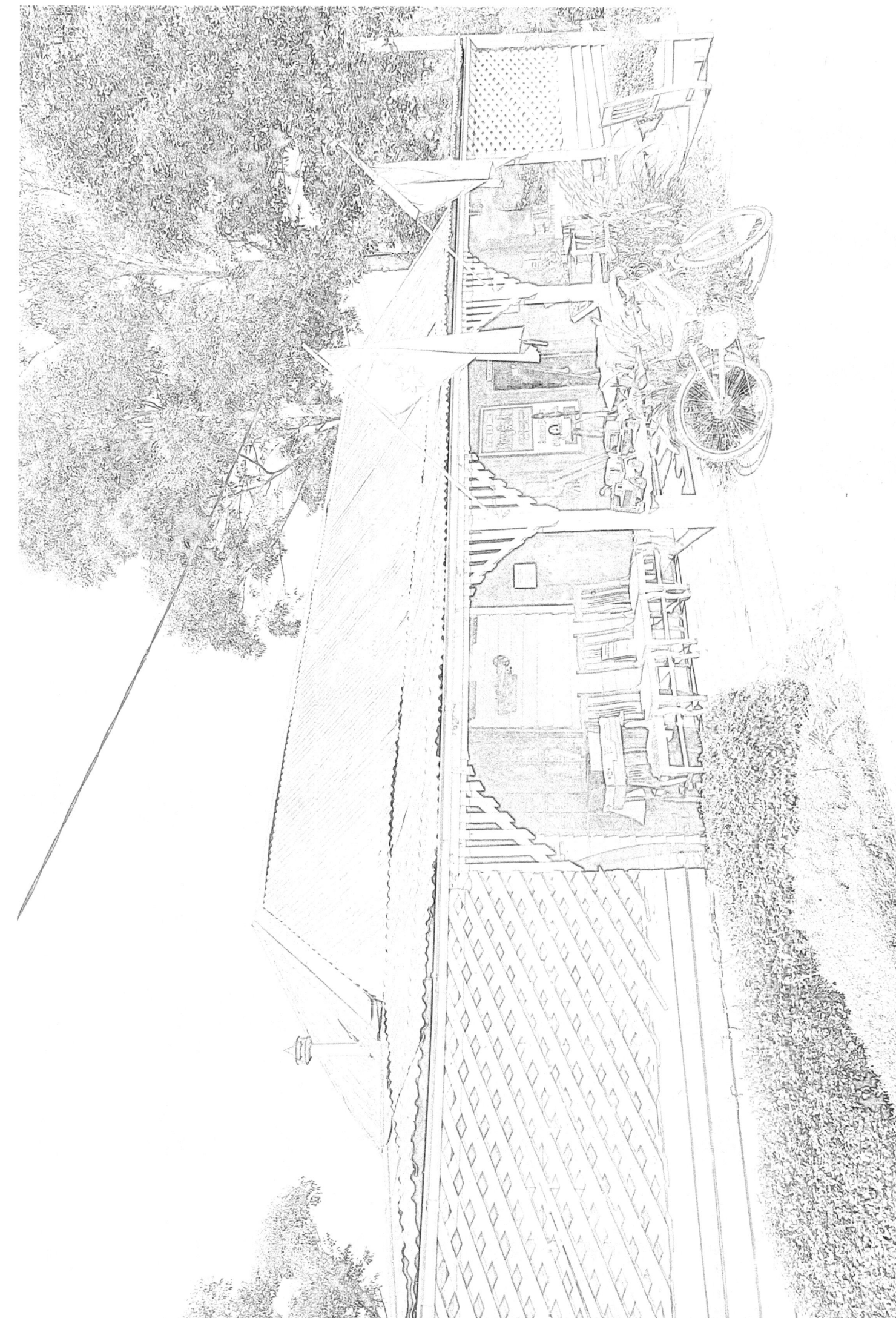

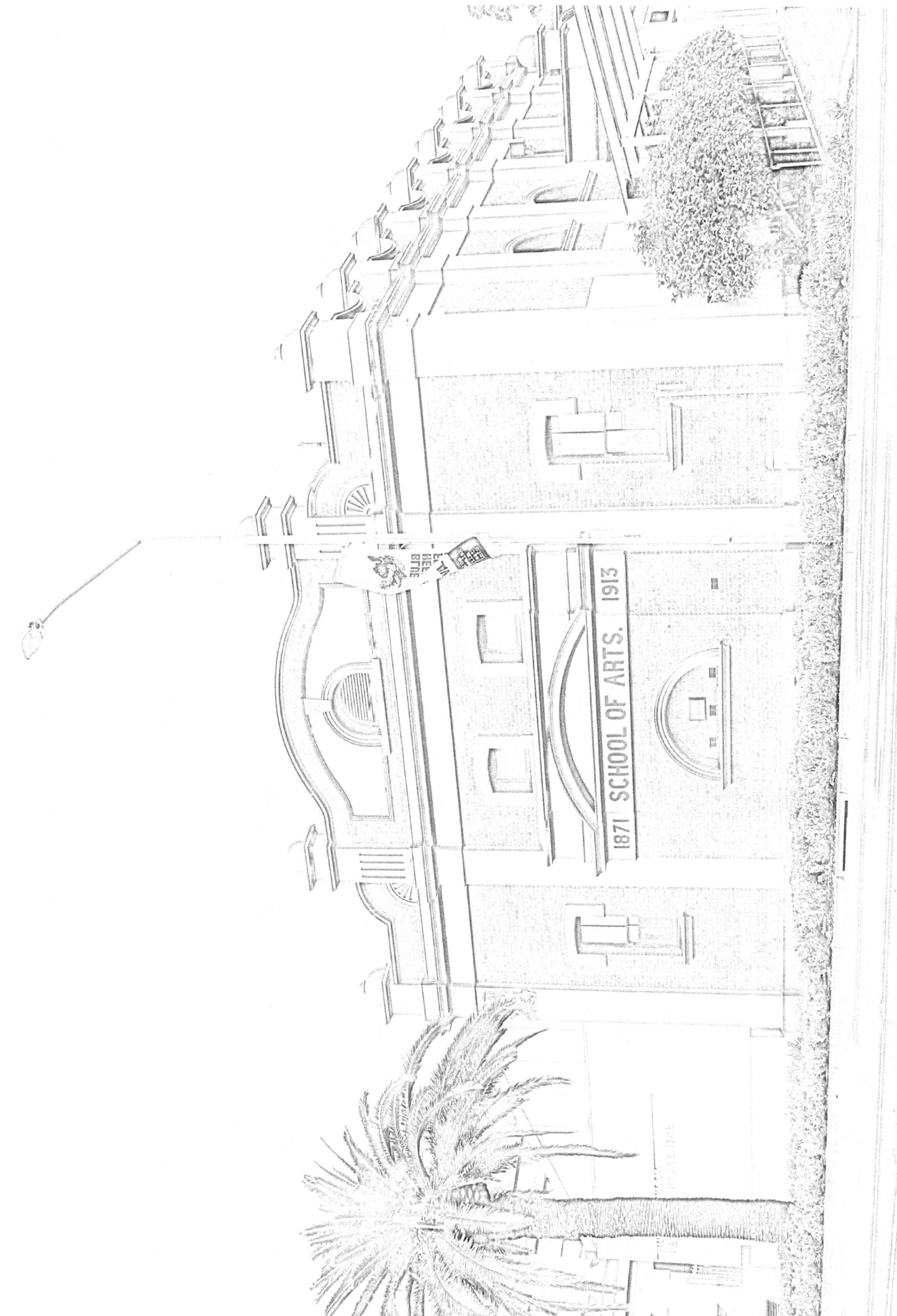

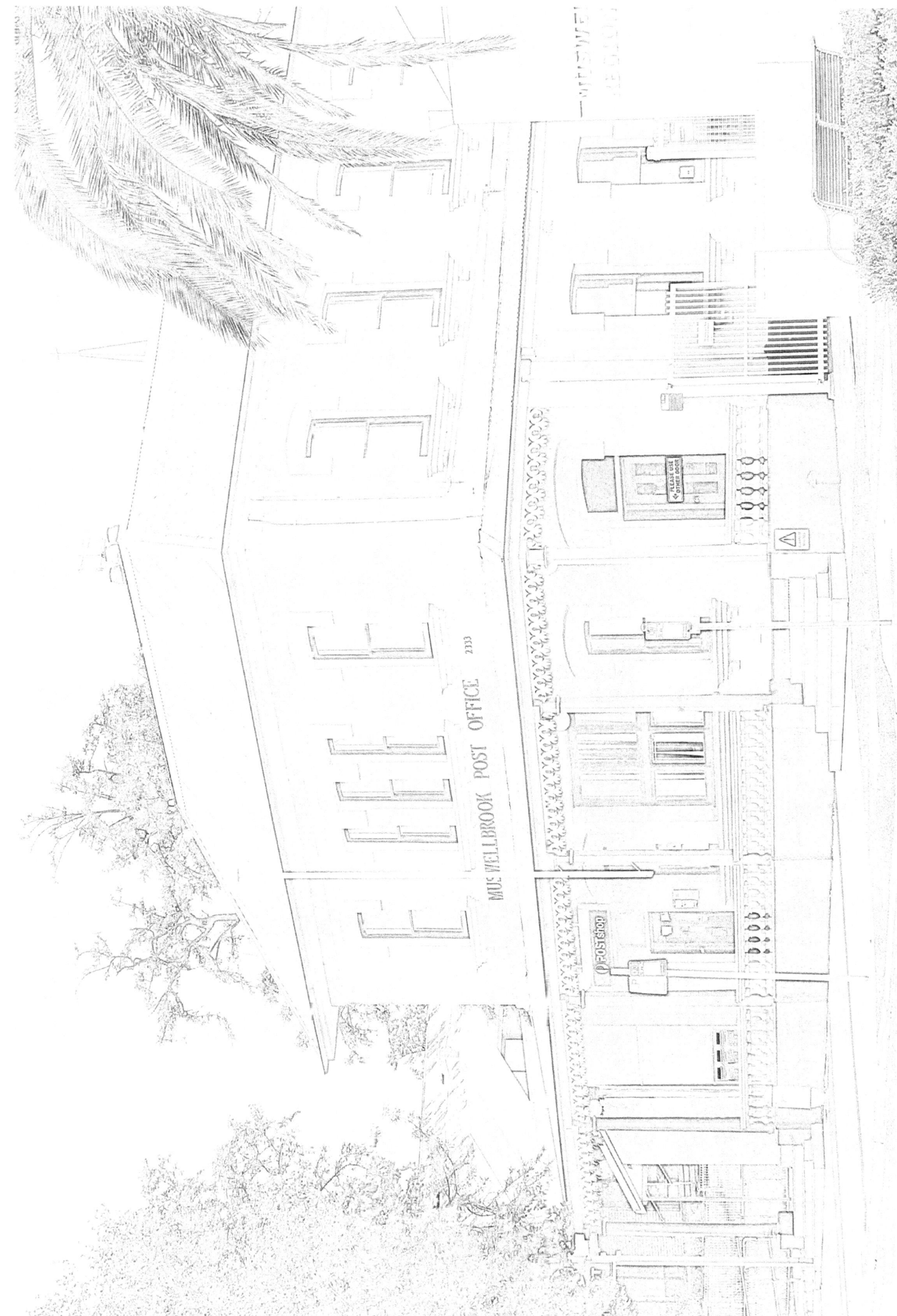

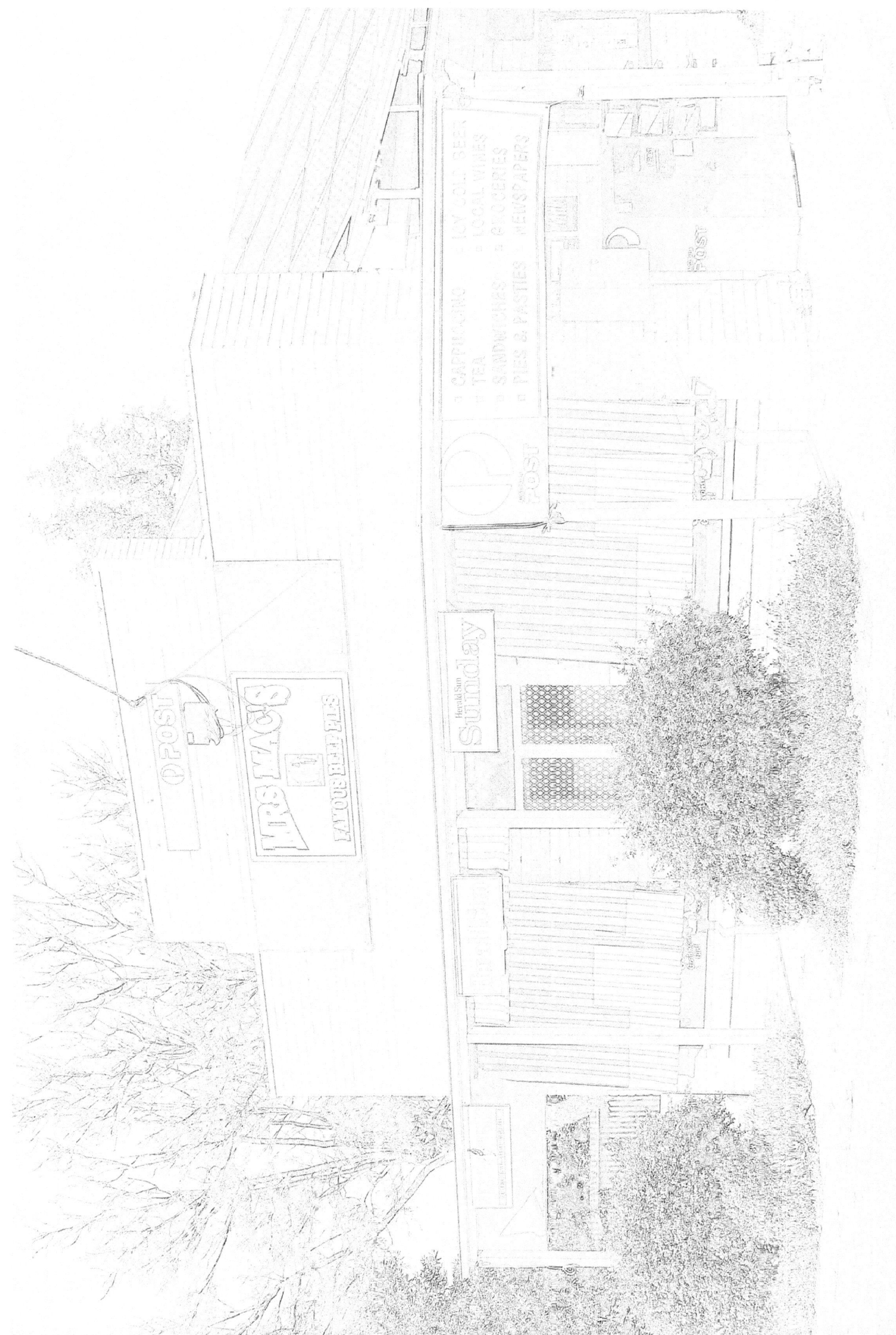

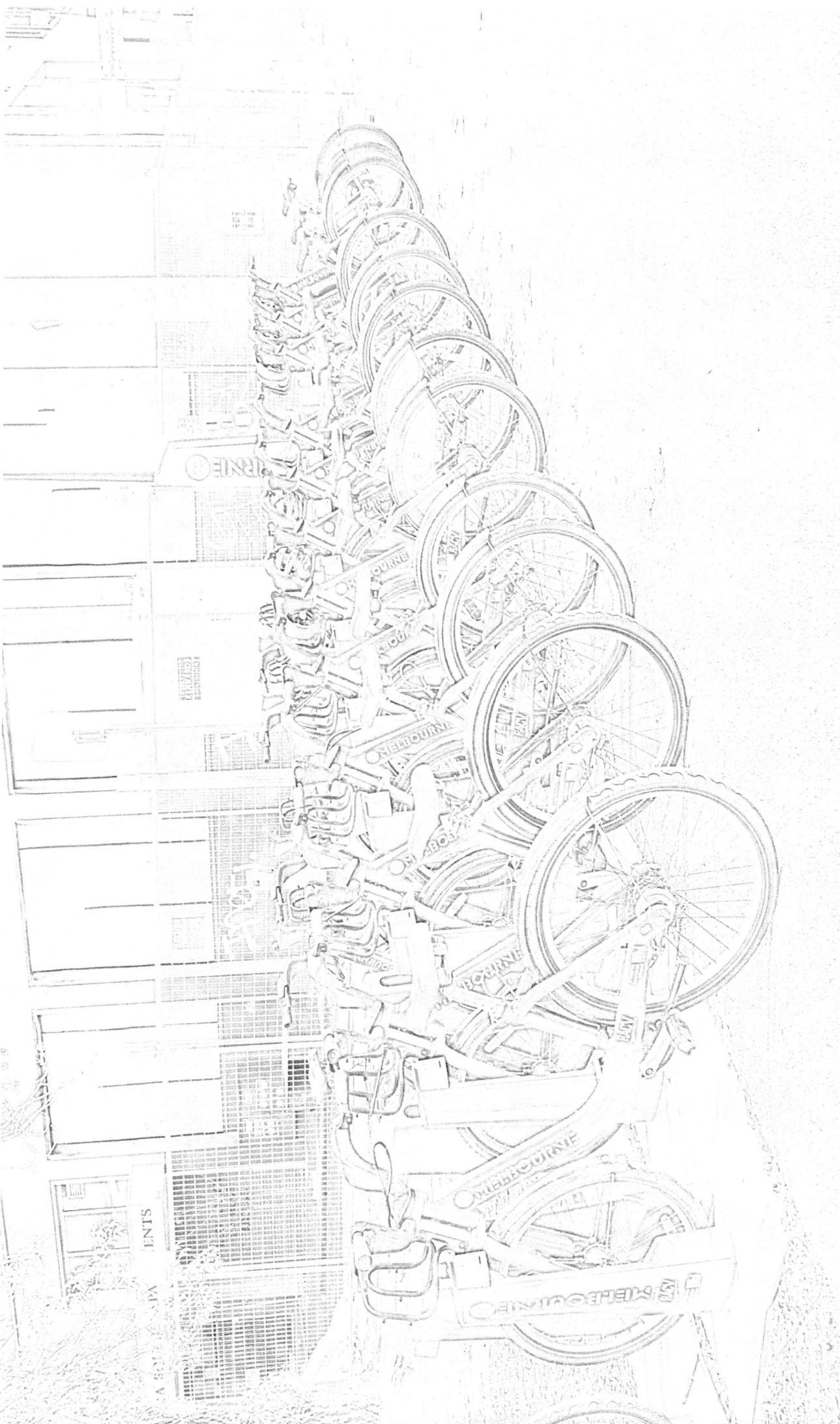

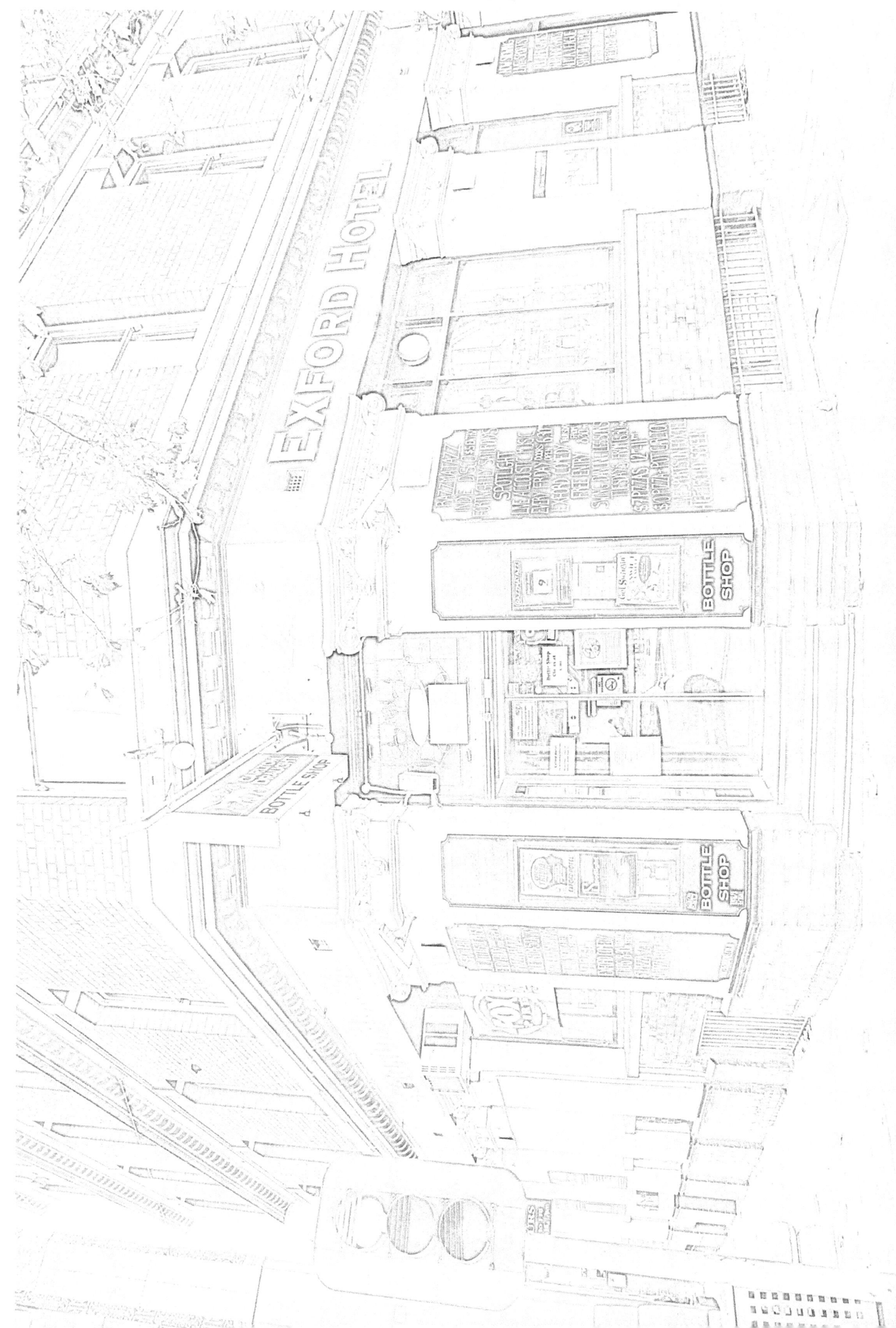

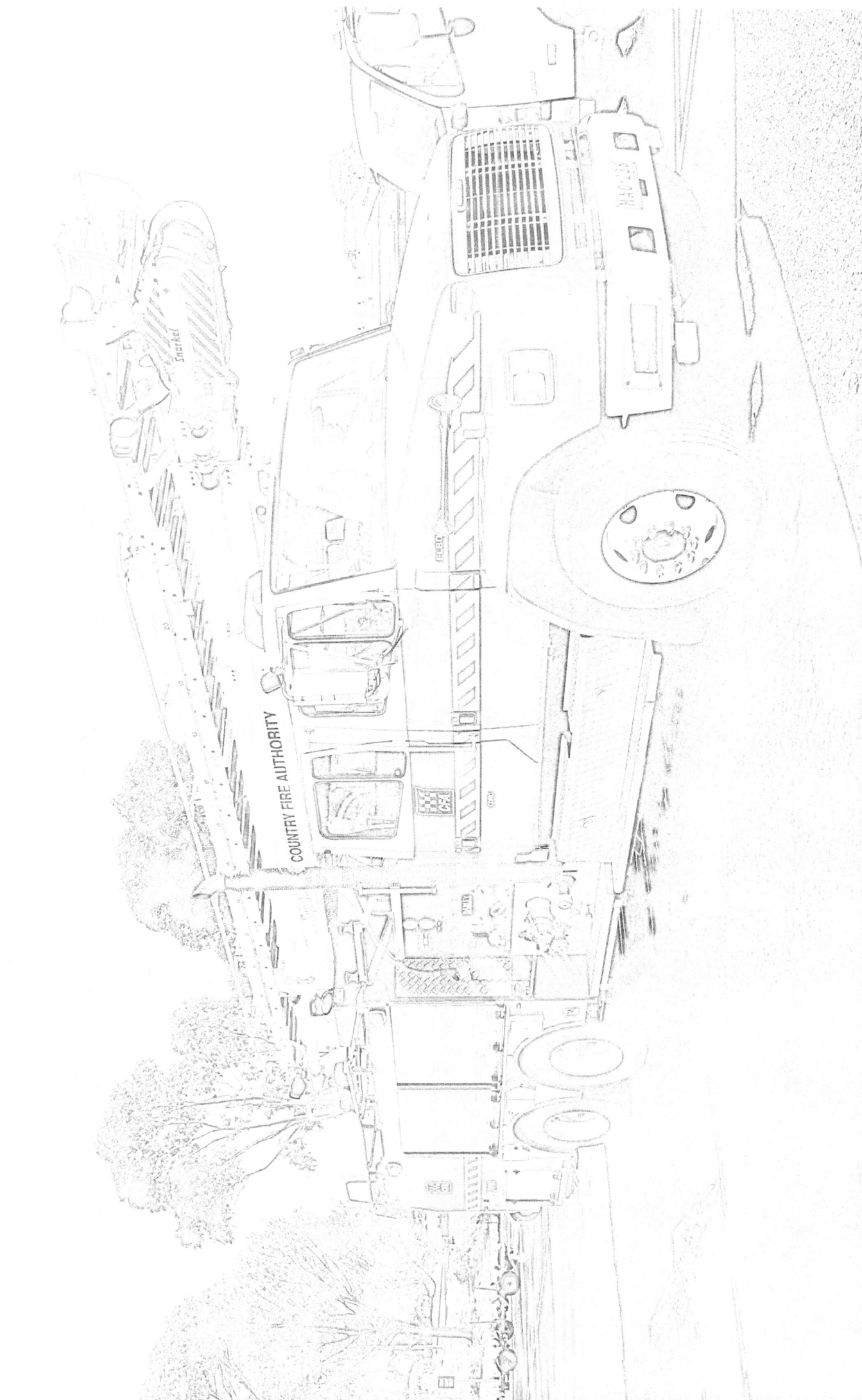

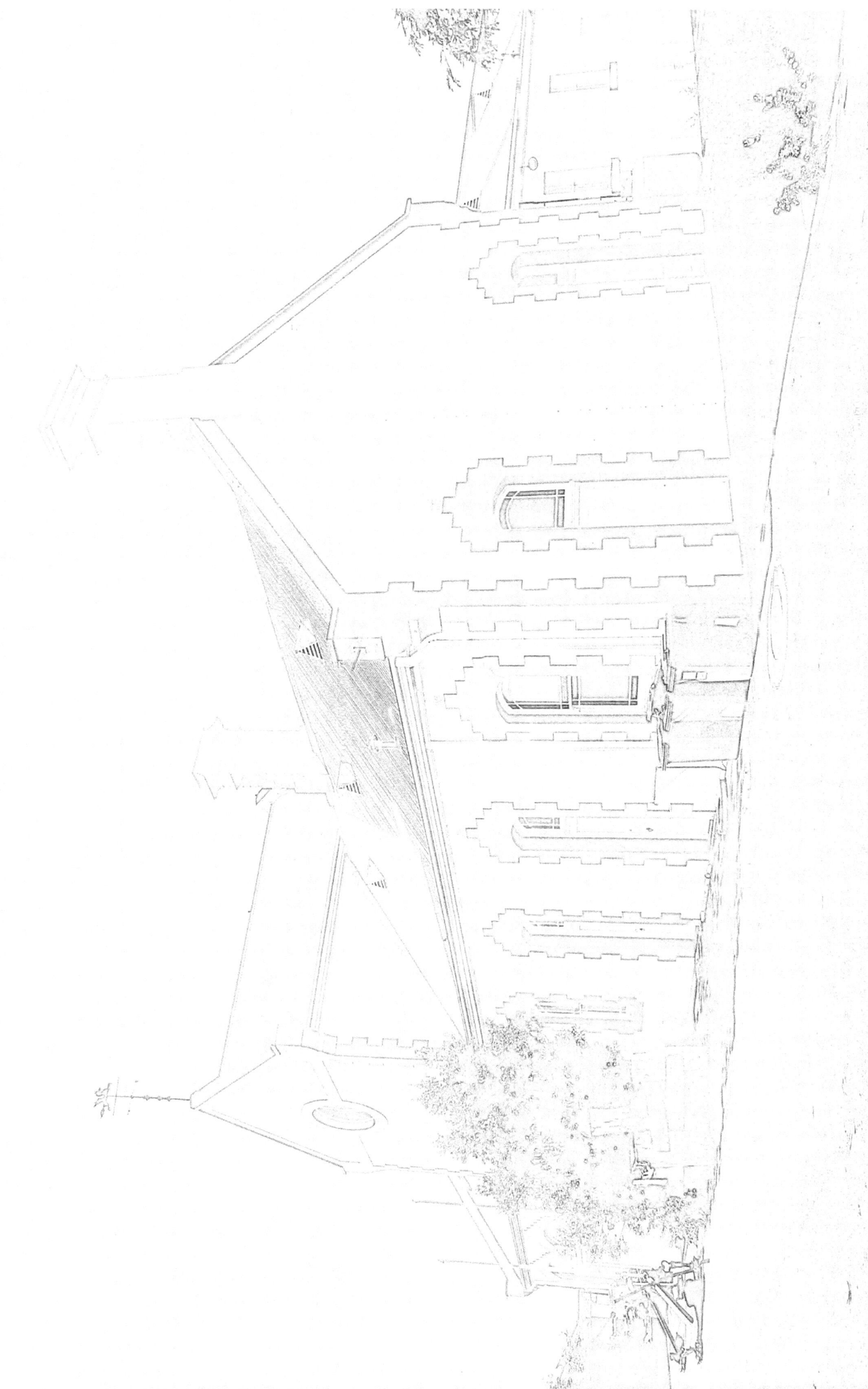

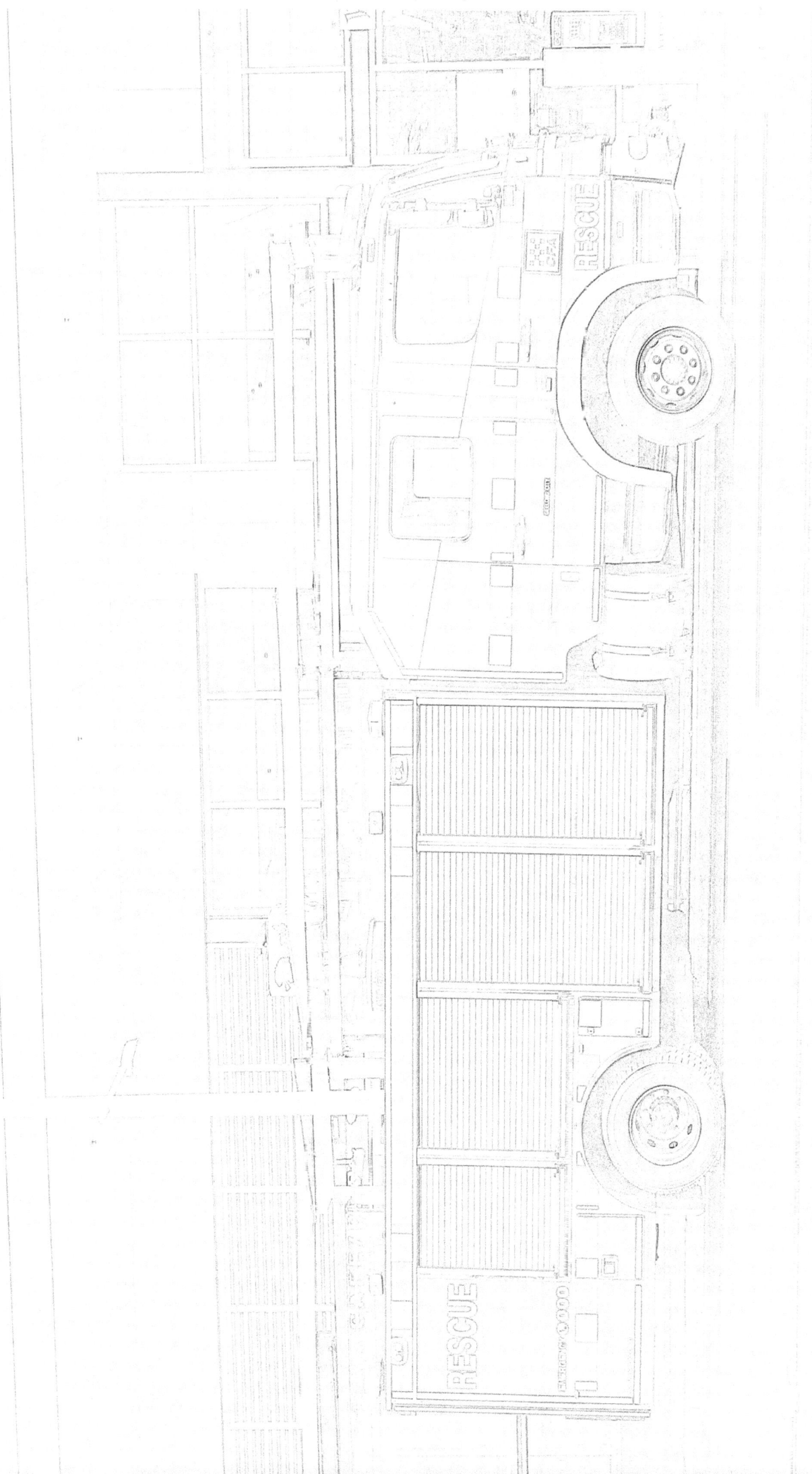

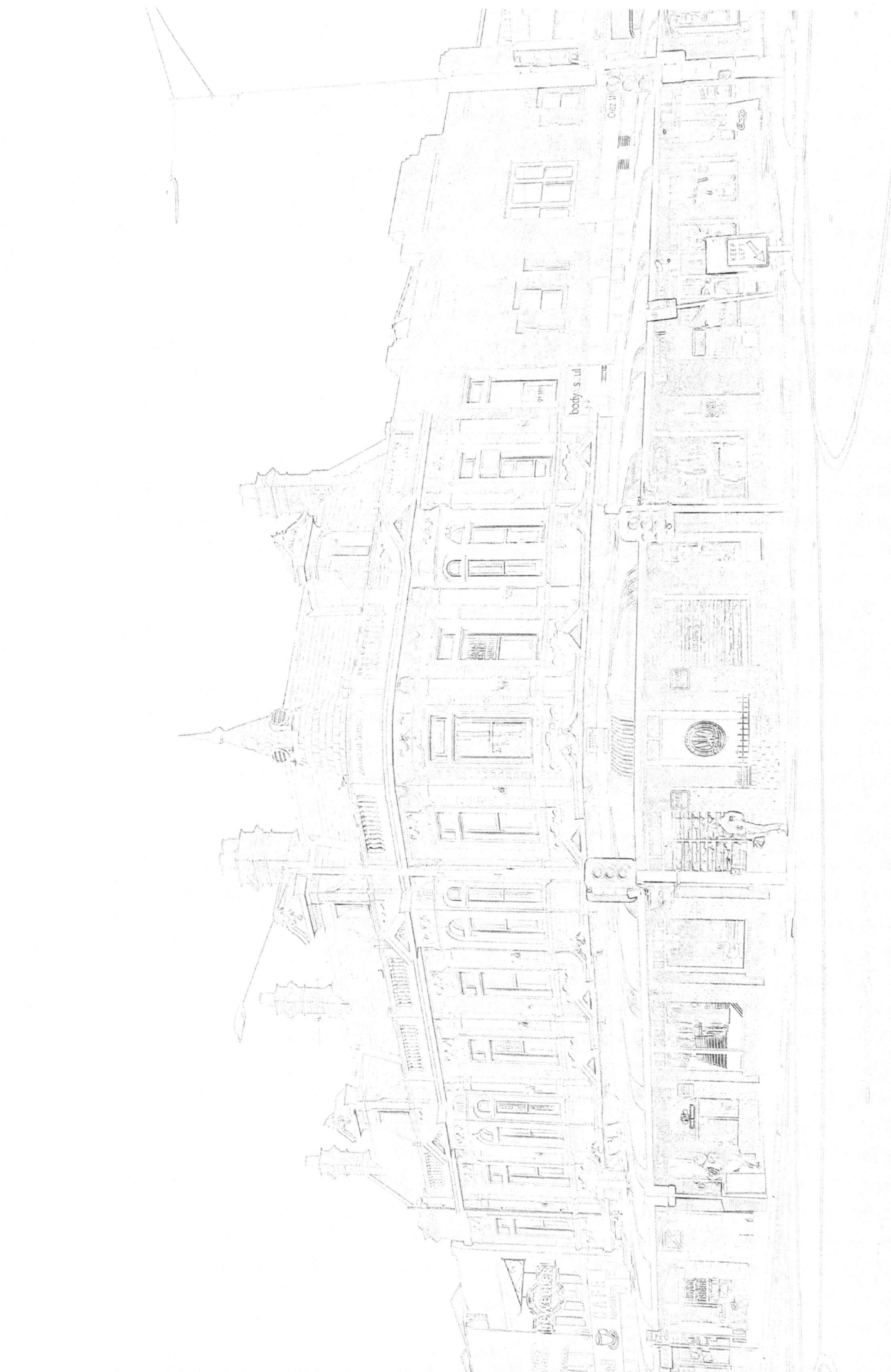

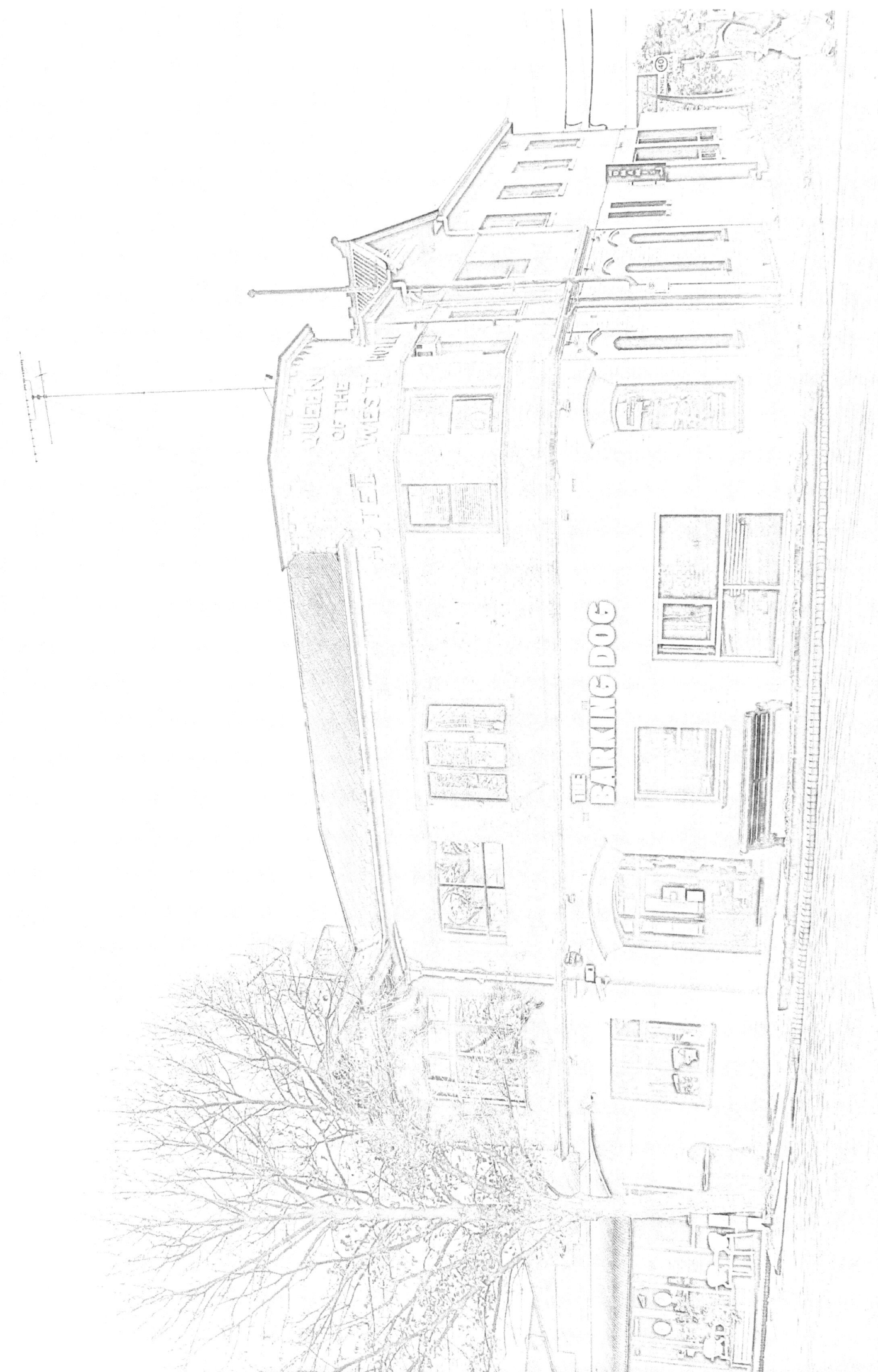

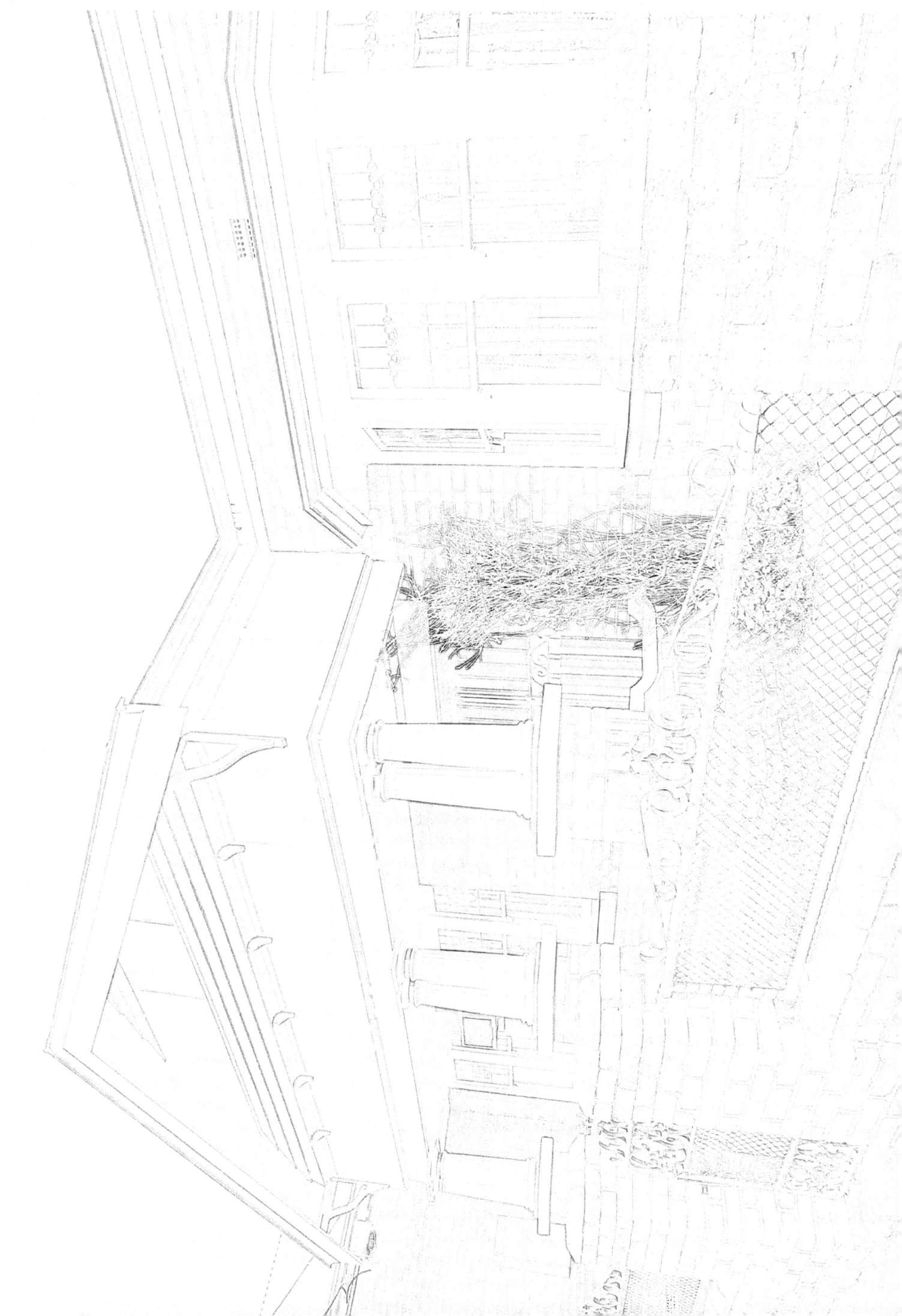

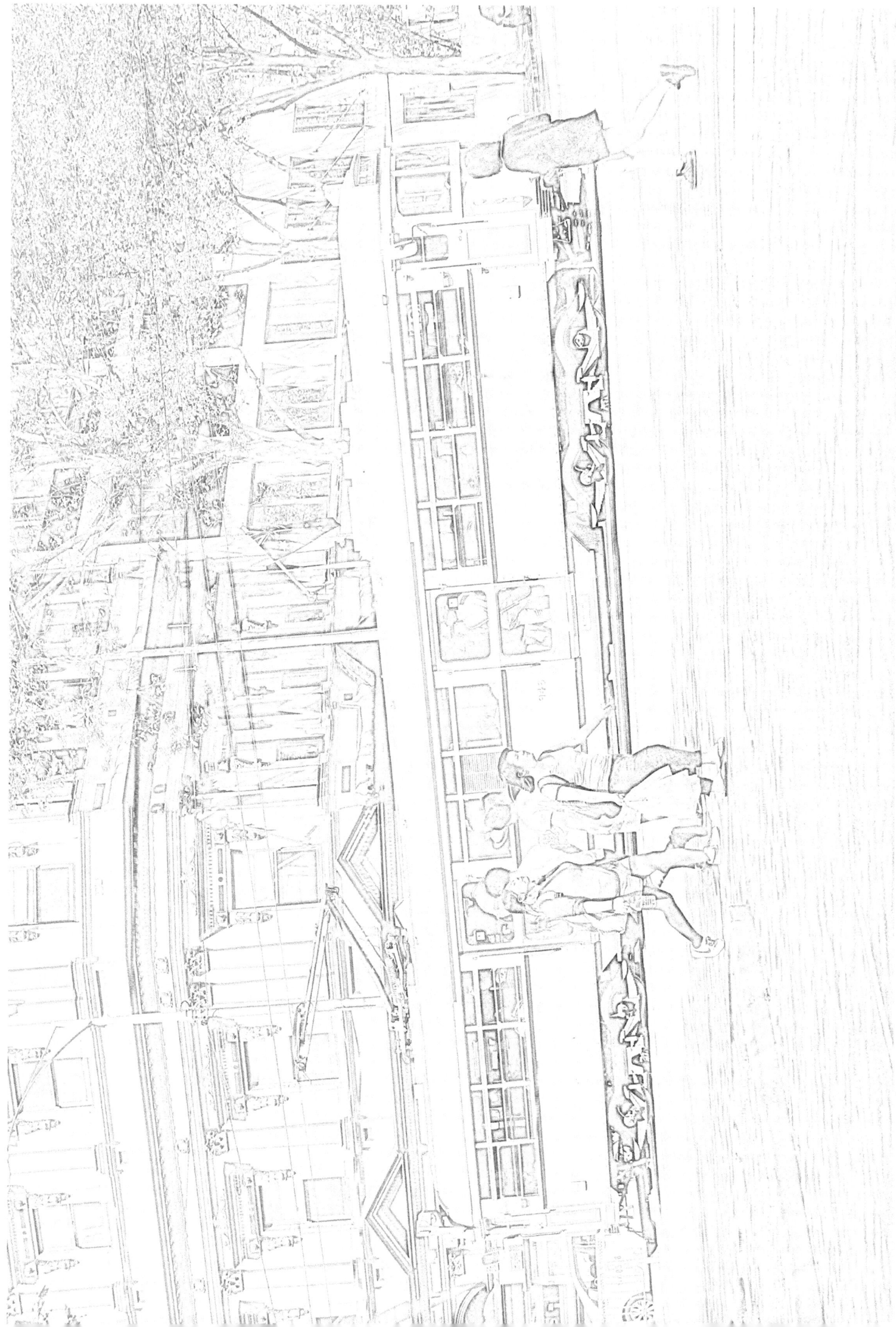

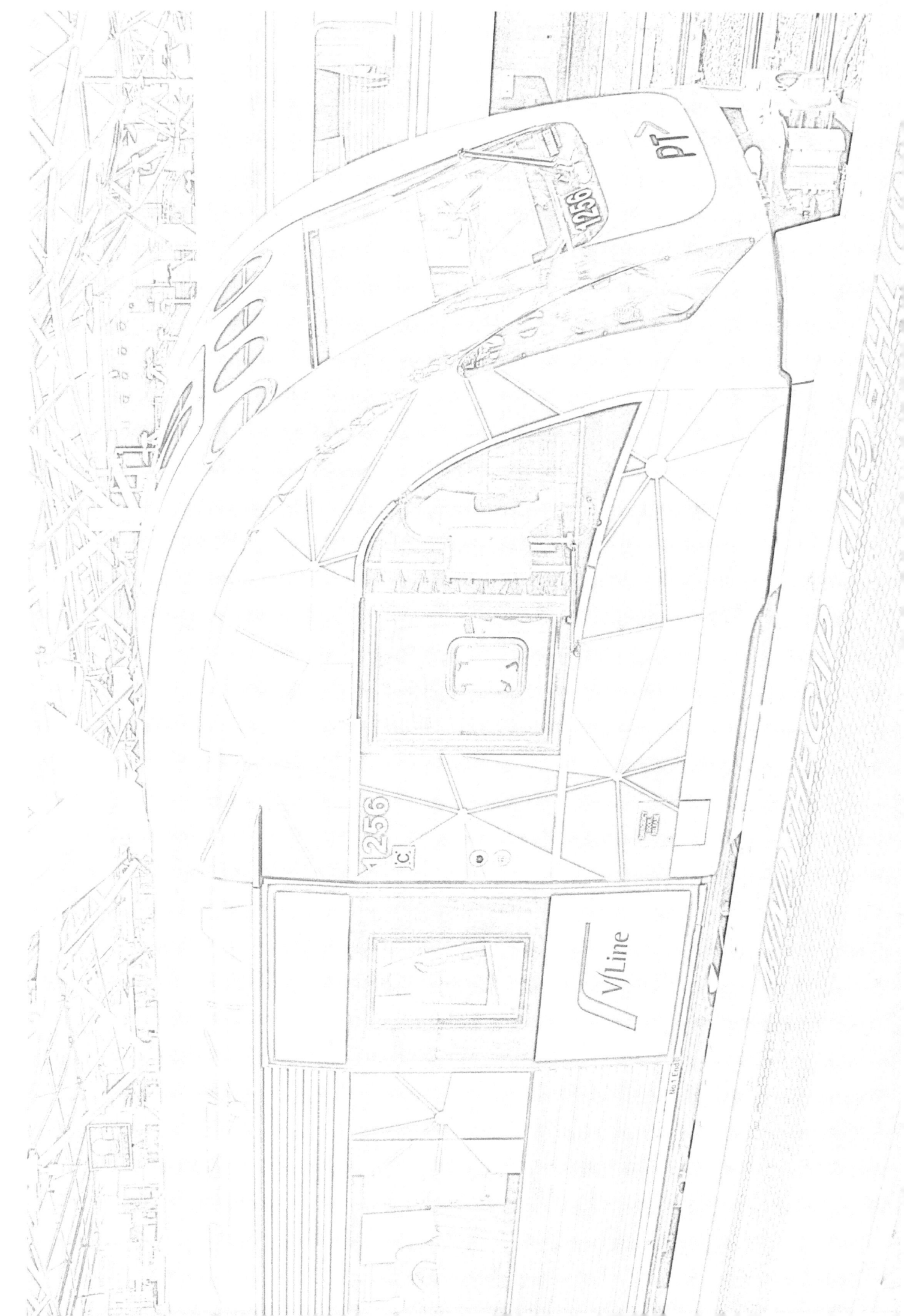

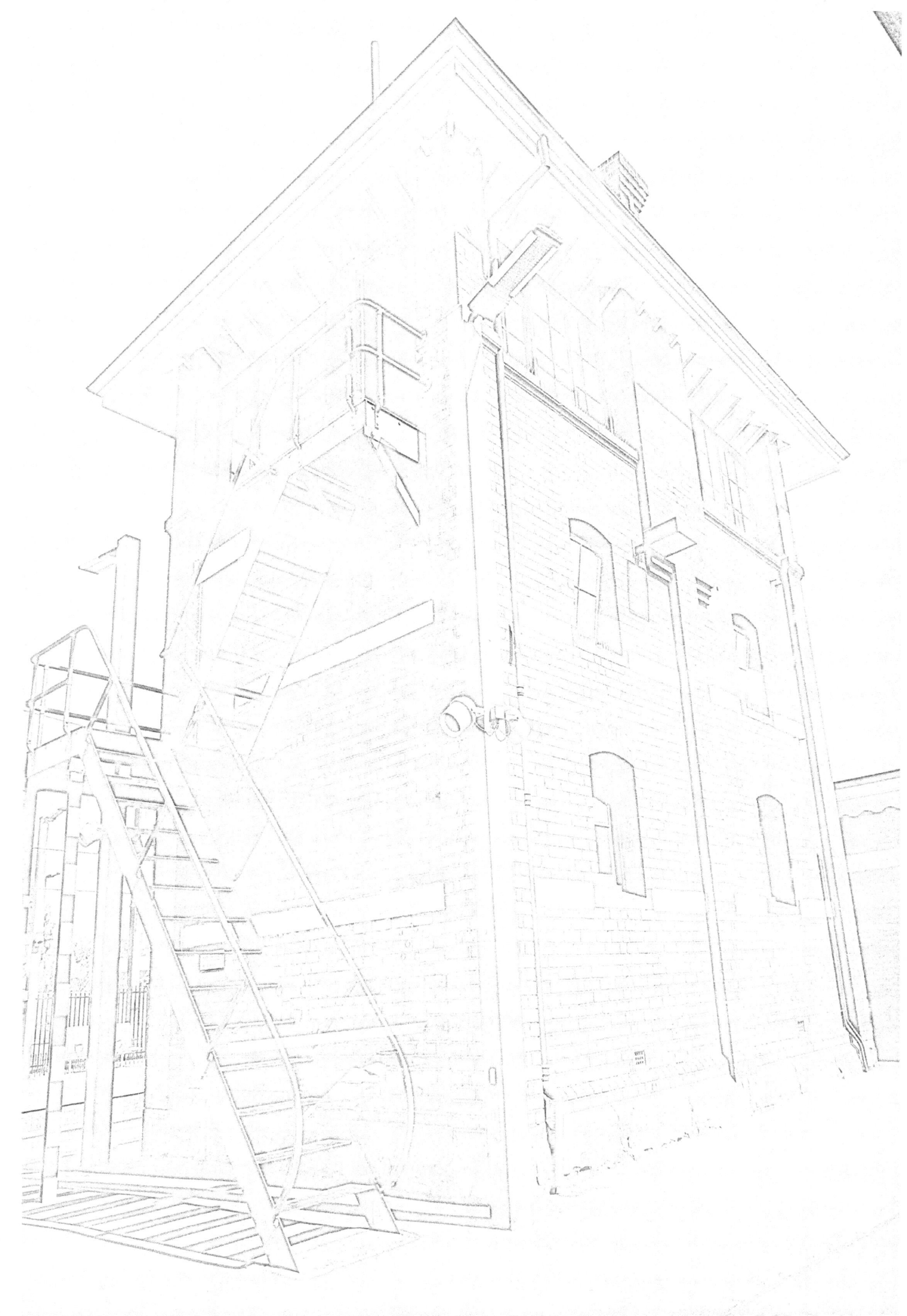

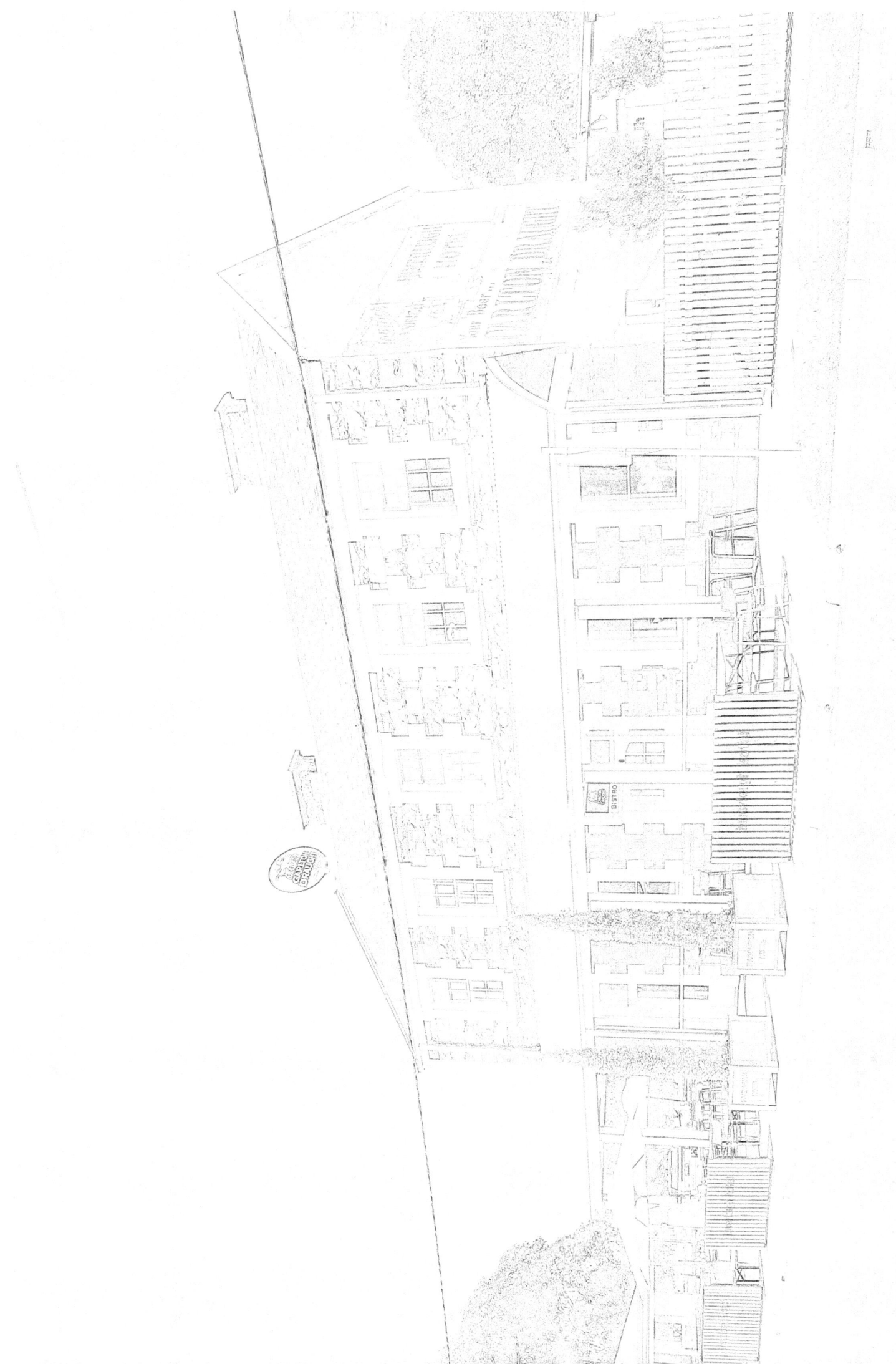

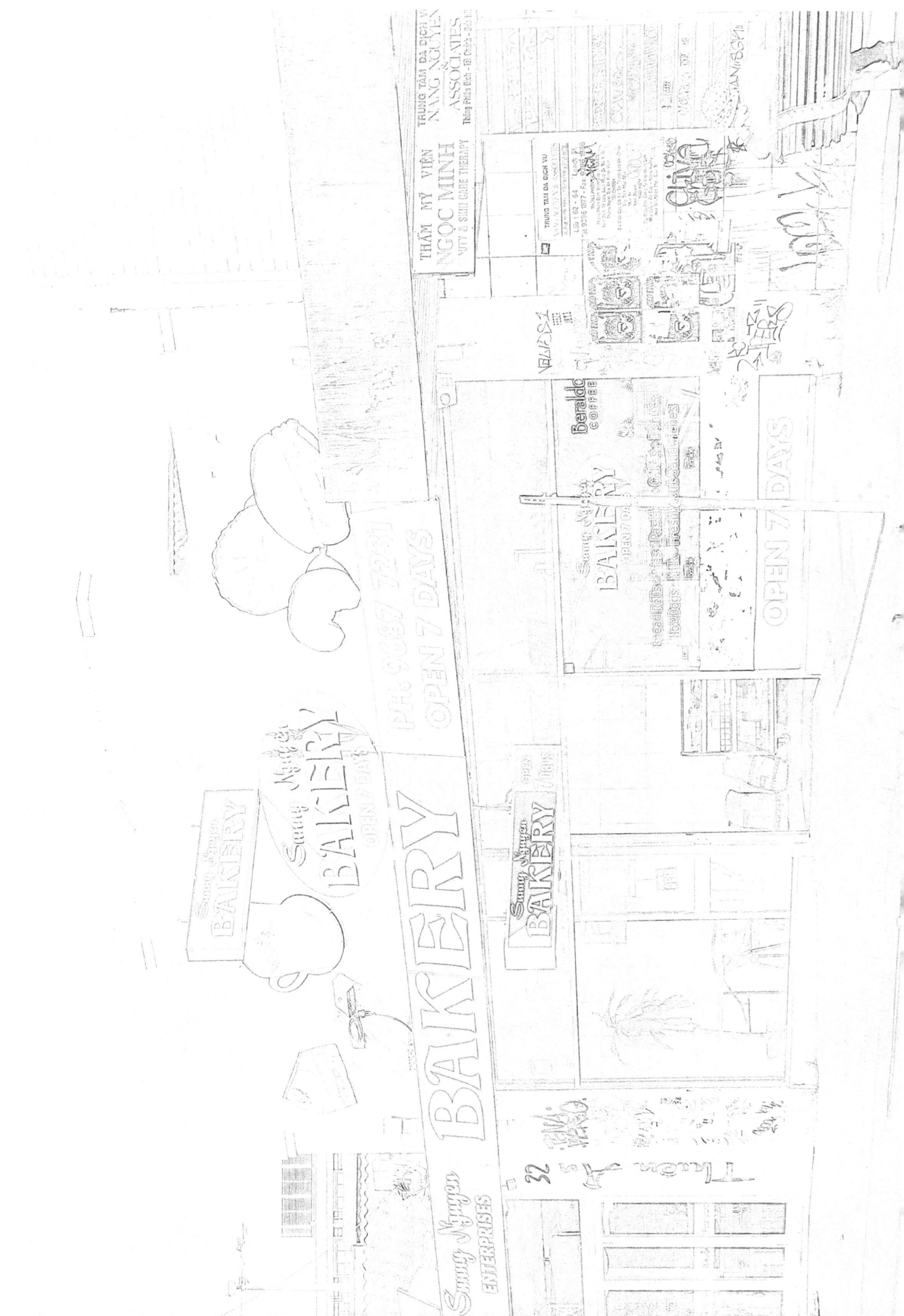

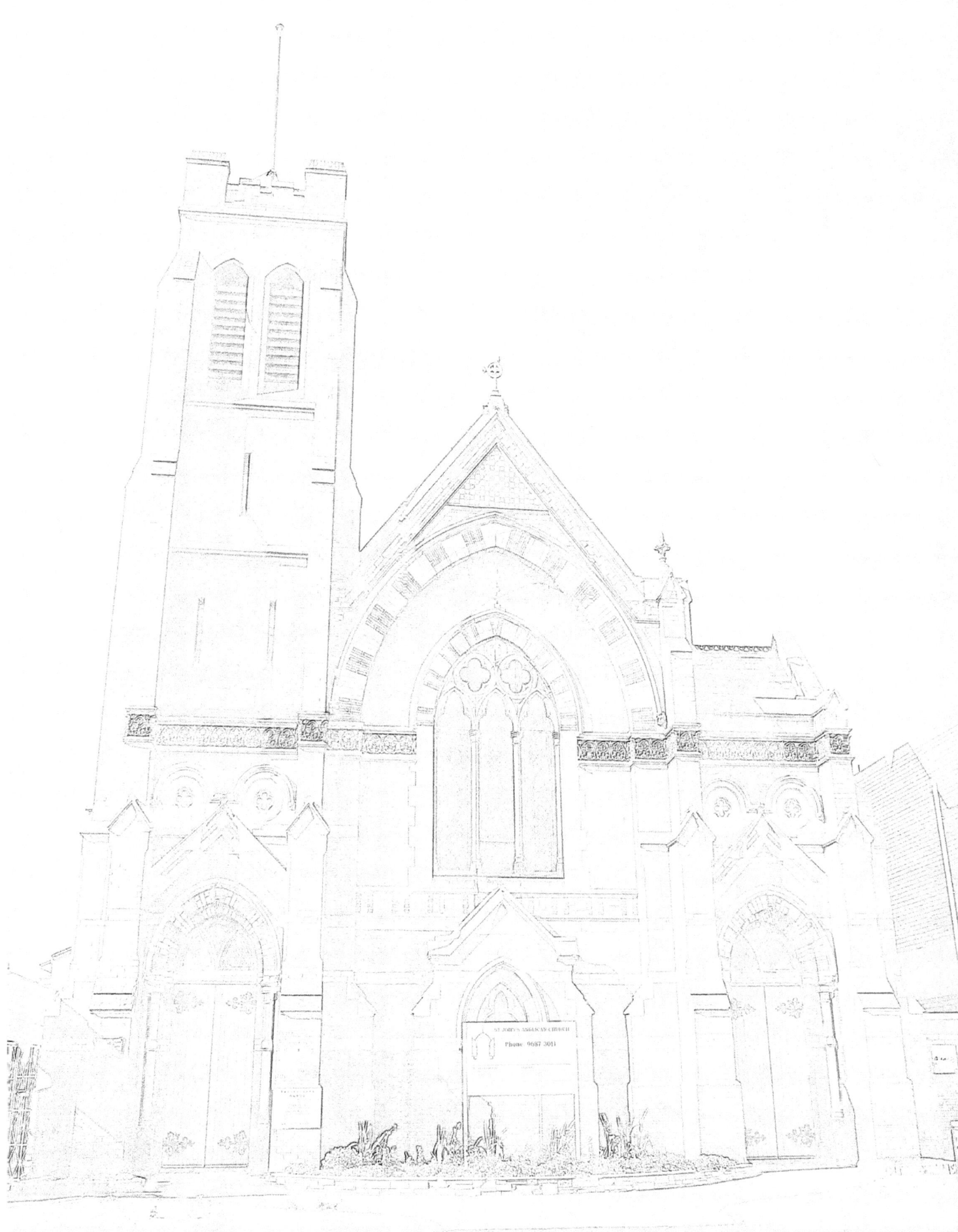

ST JOHN'S ANGLICAN CHURCH
Phone 9687 3011

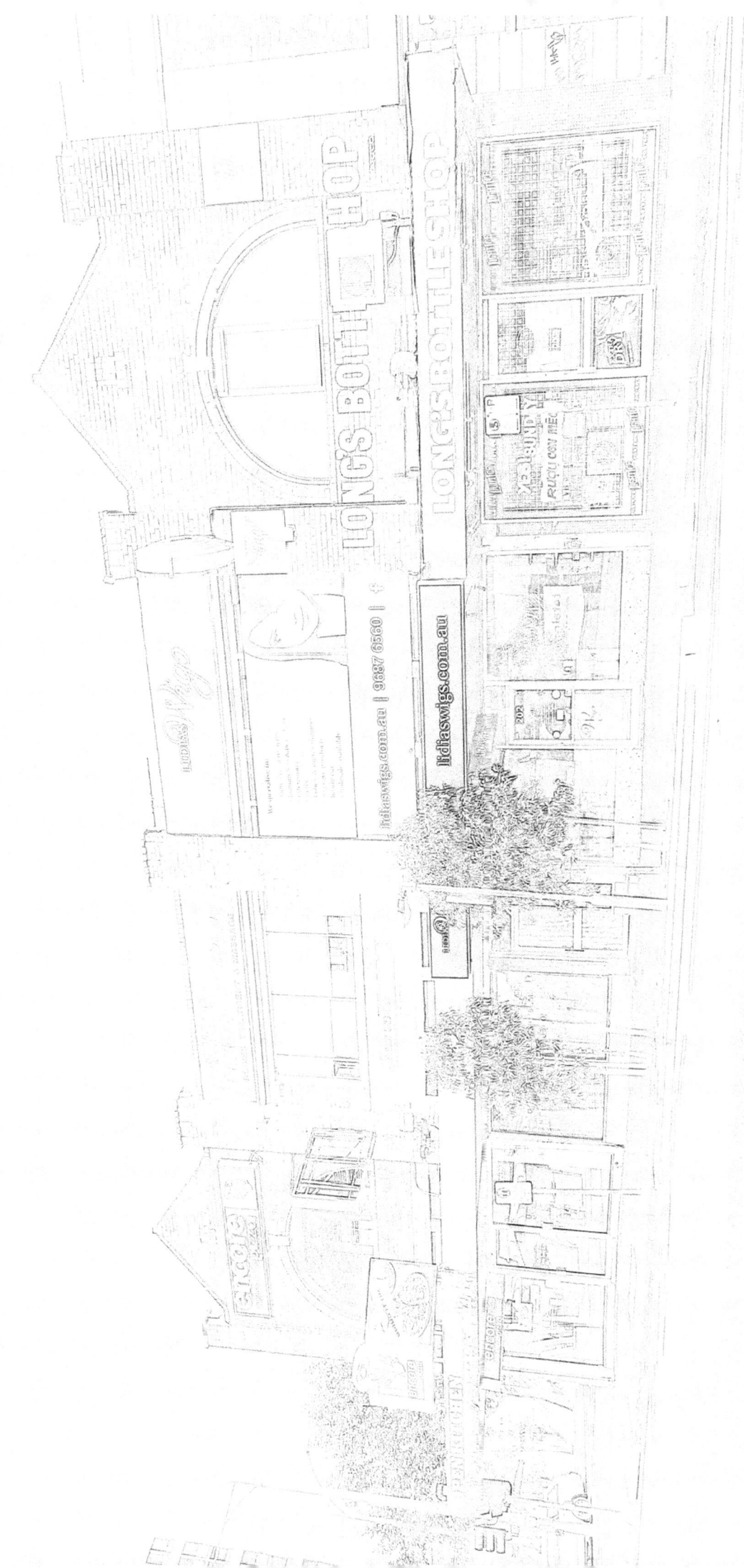

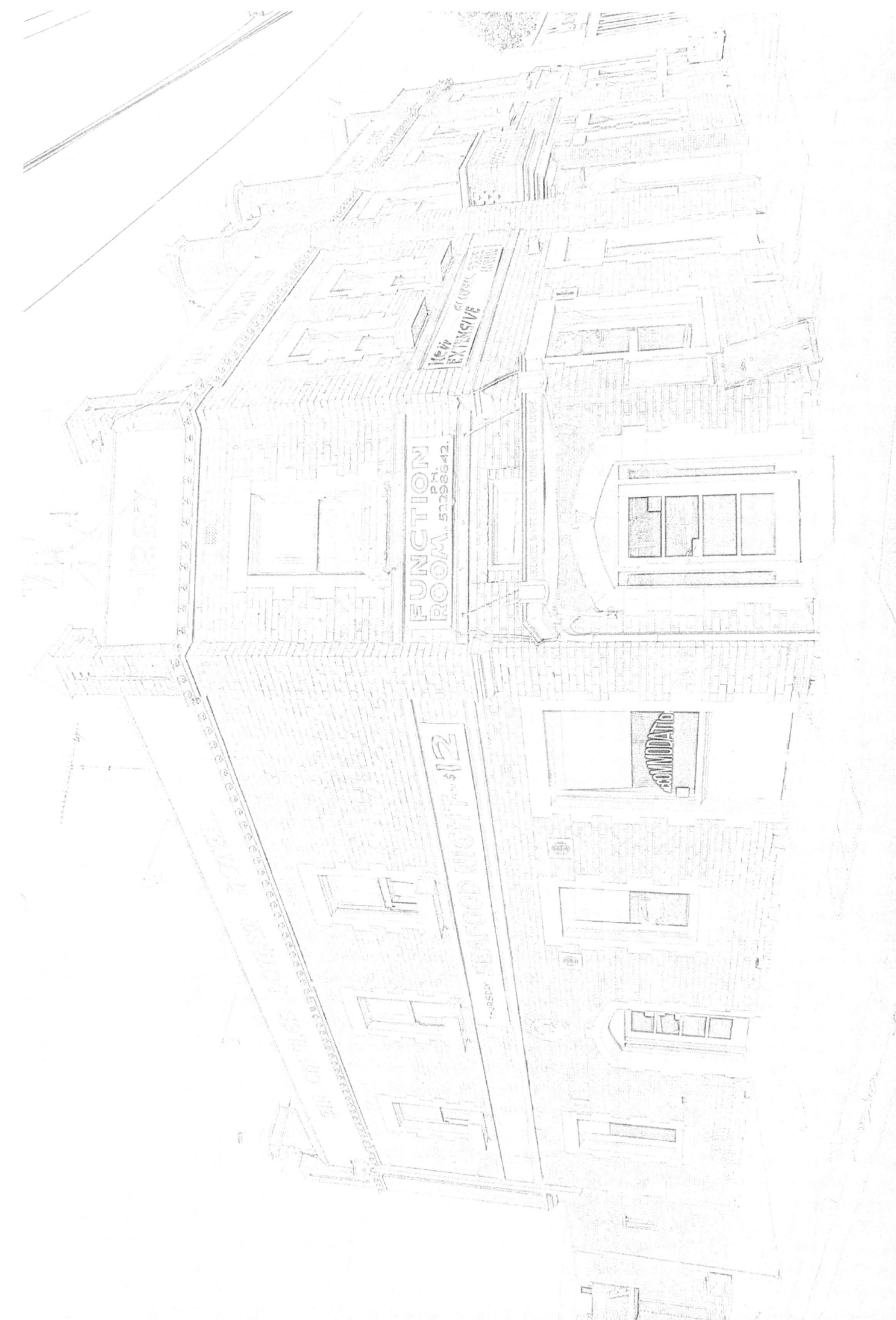

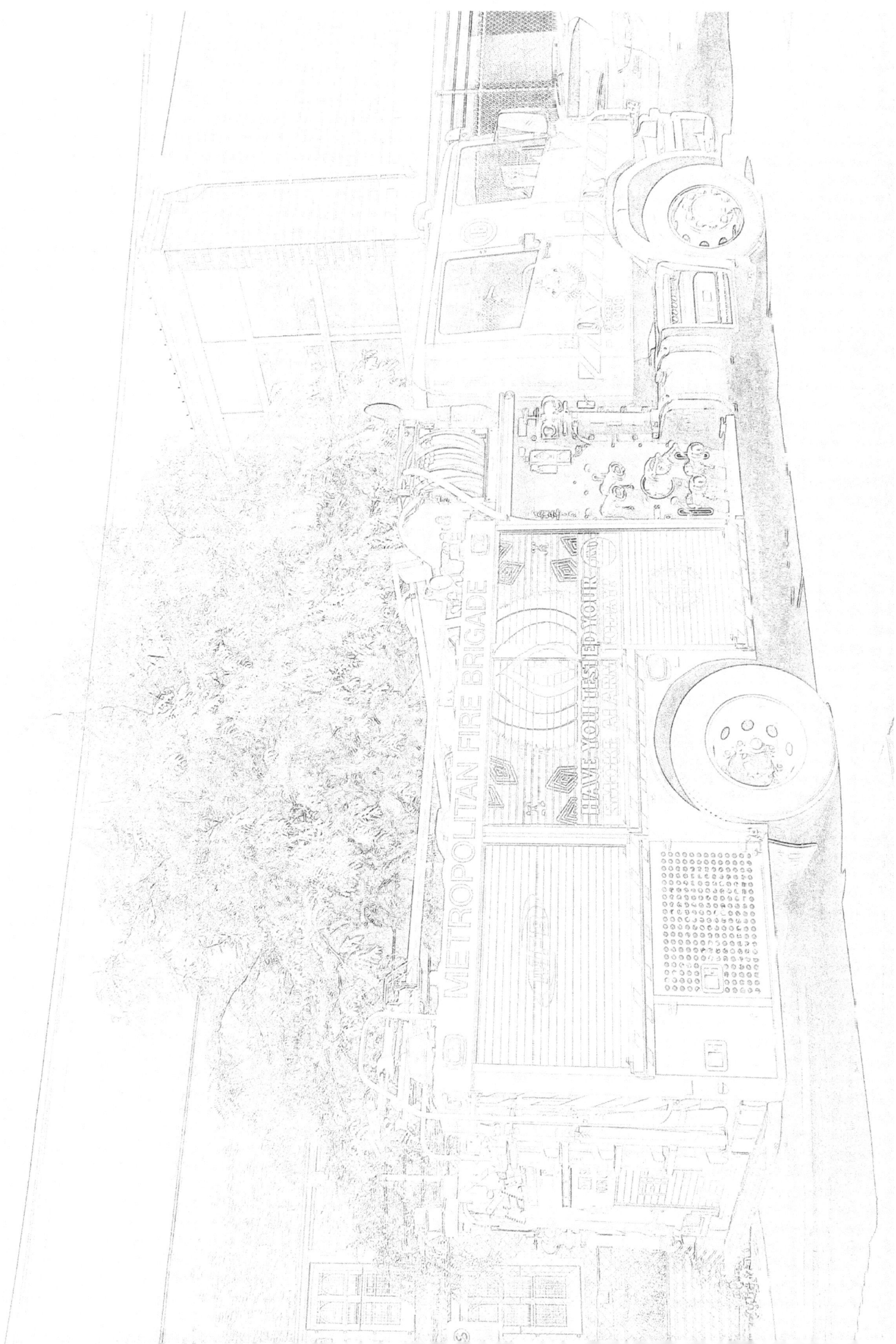

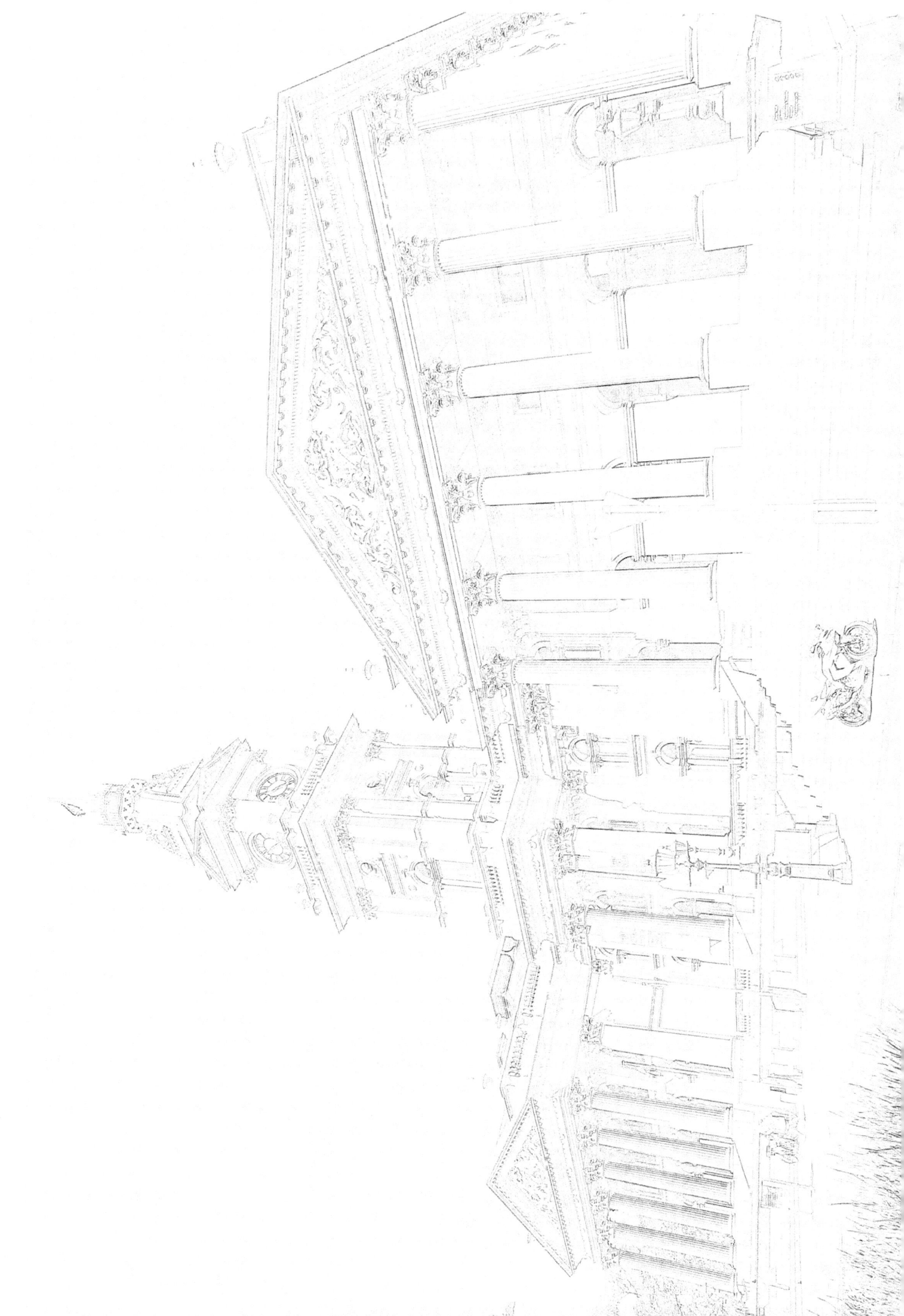

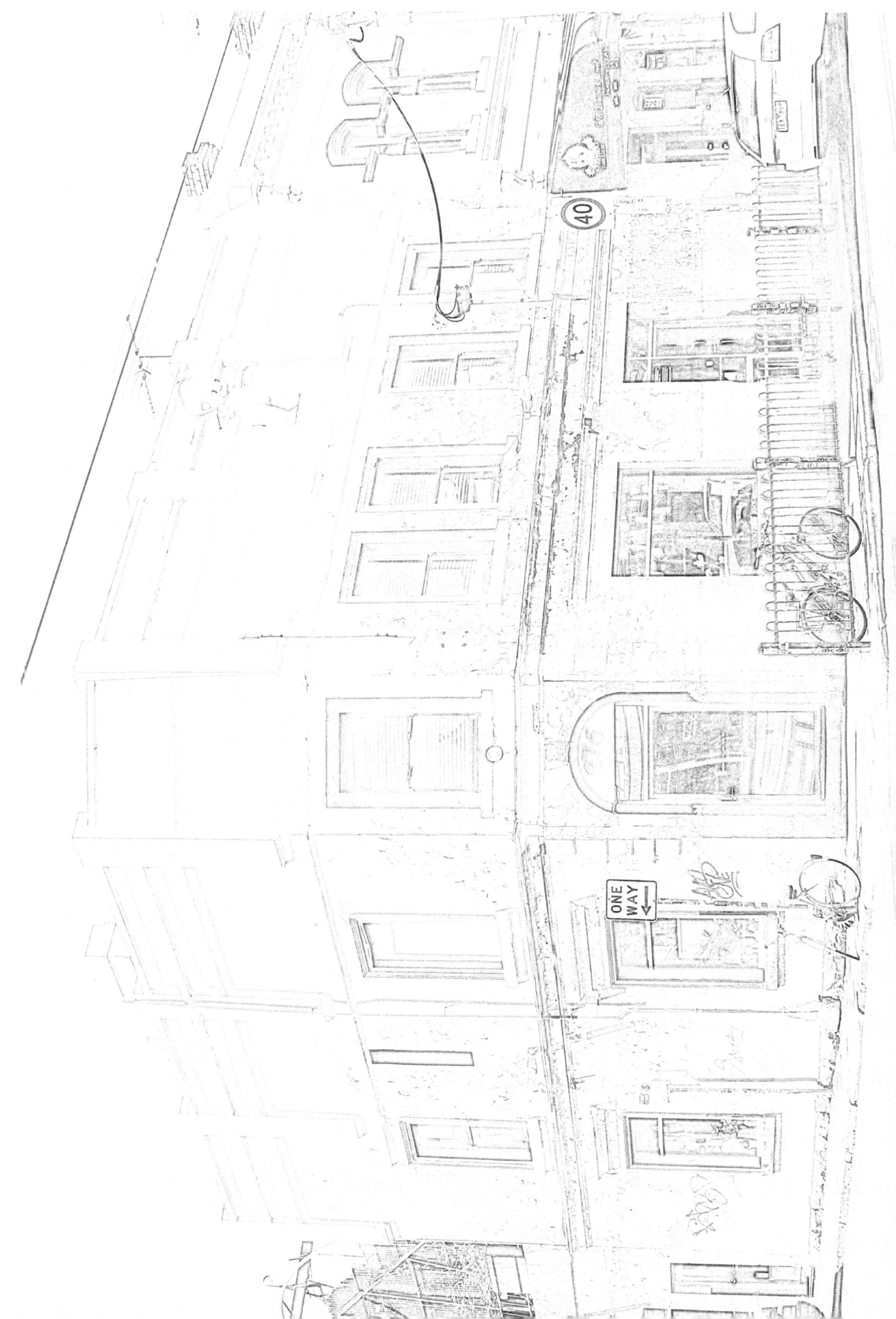

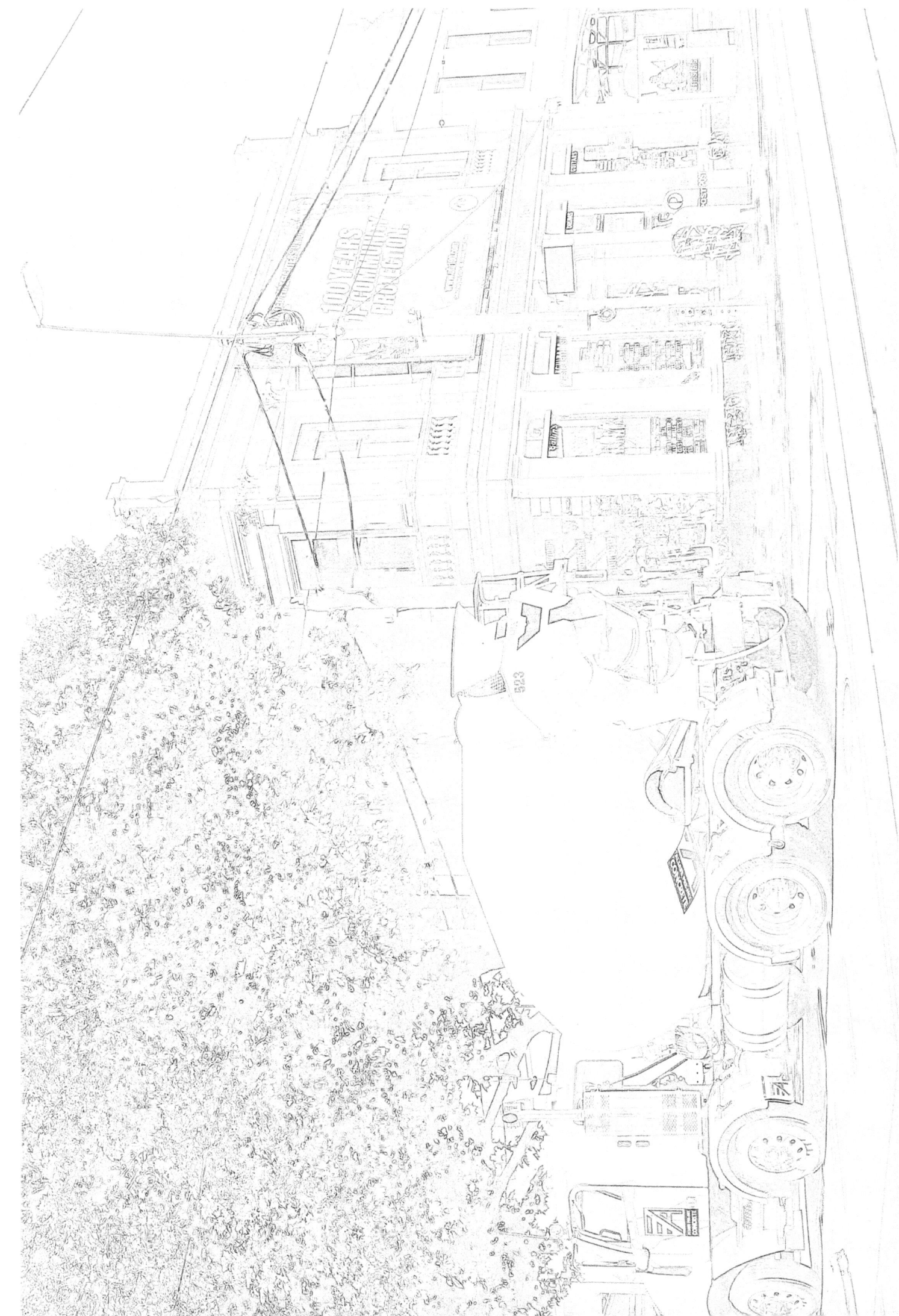

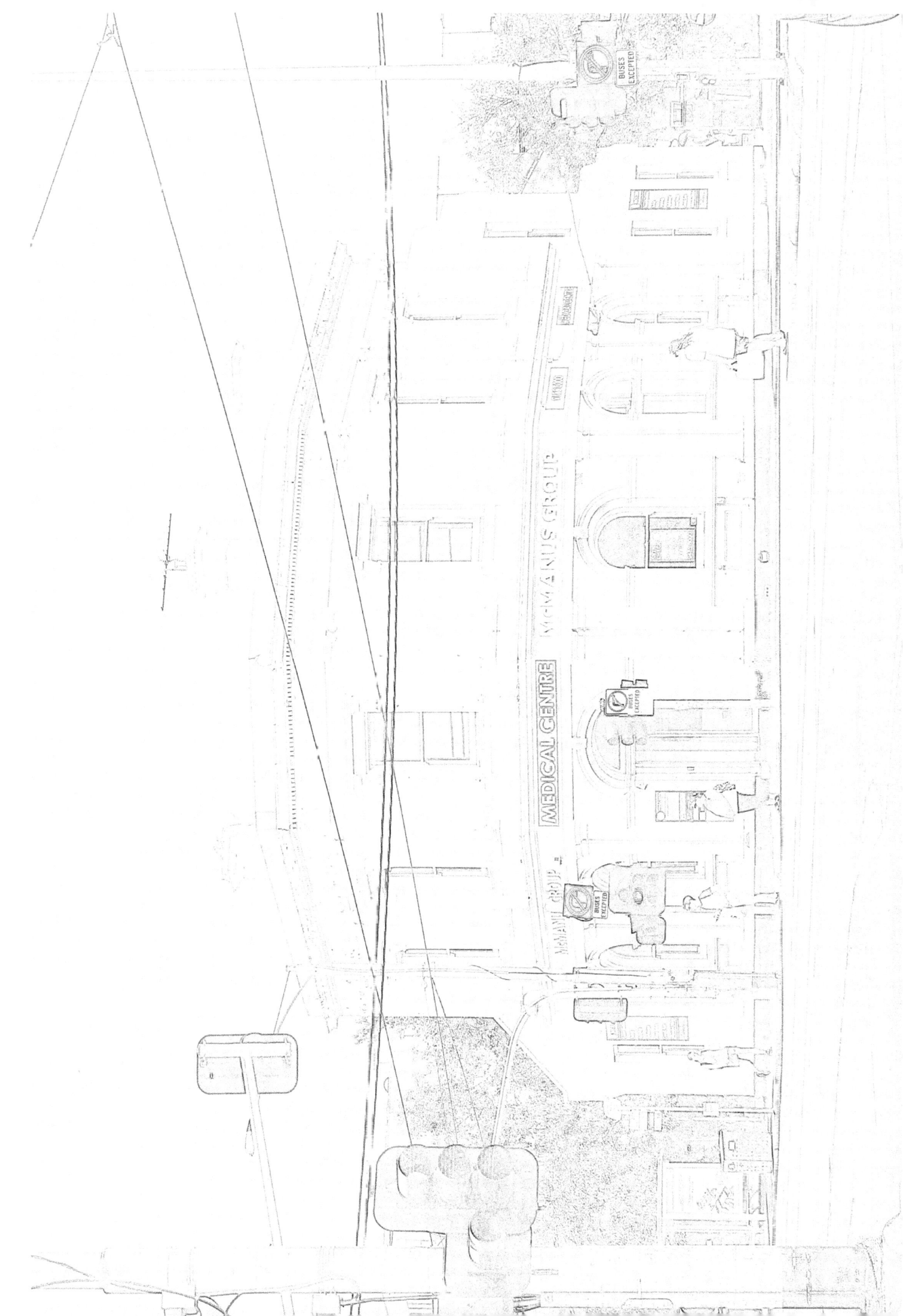

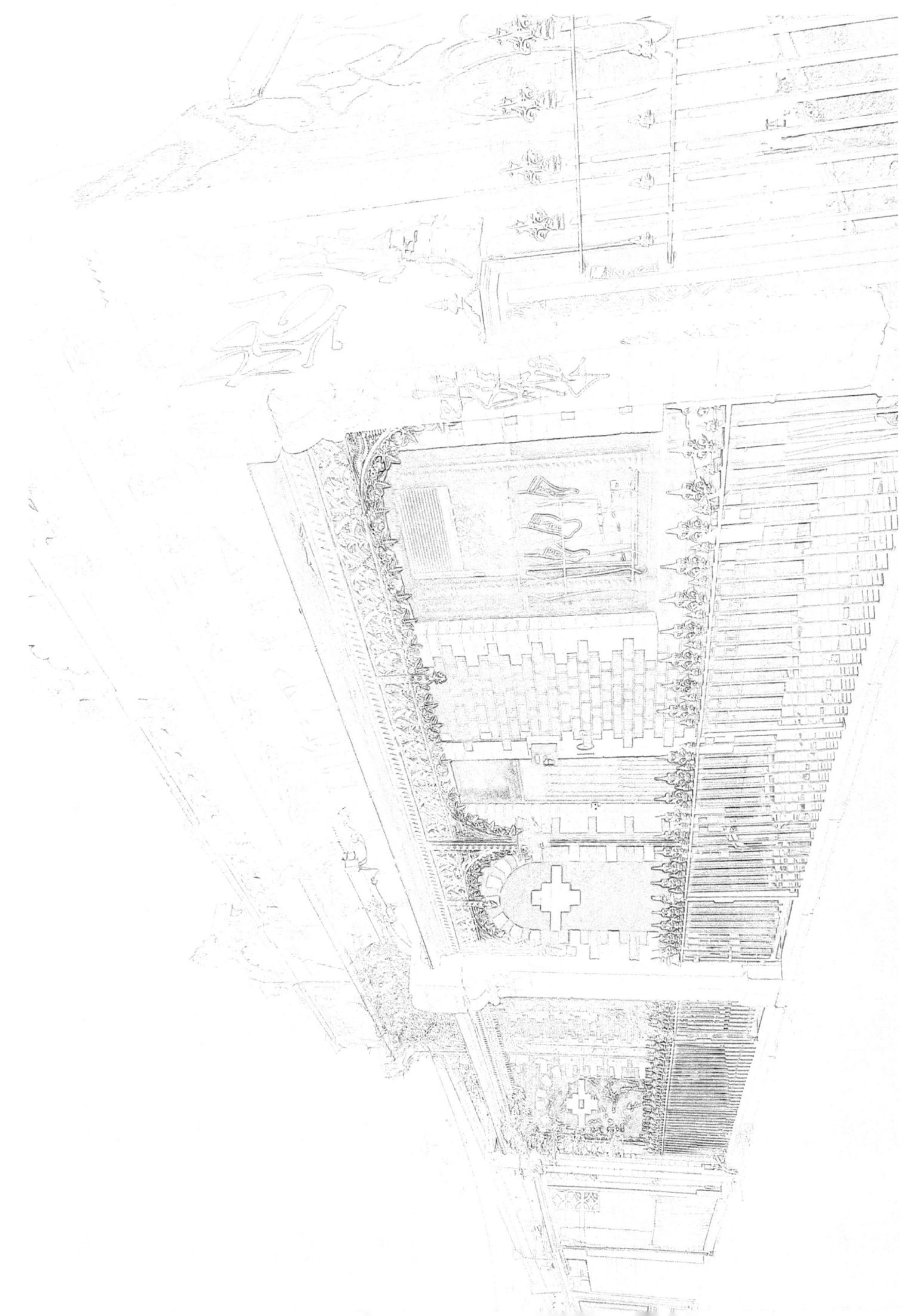

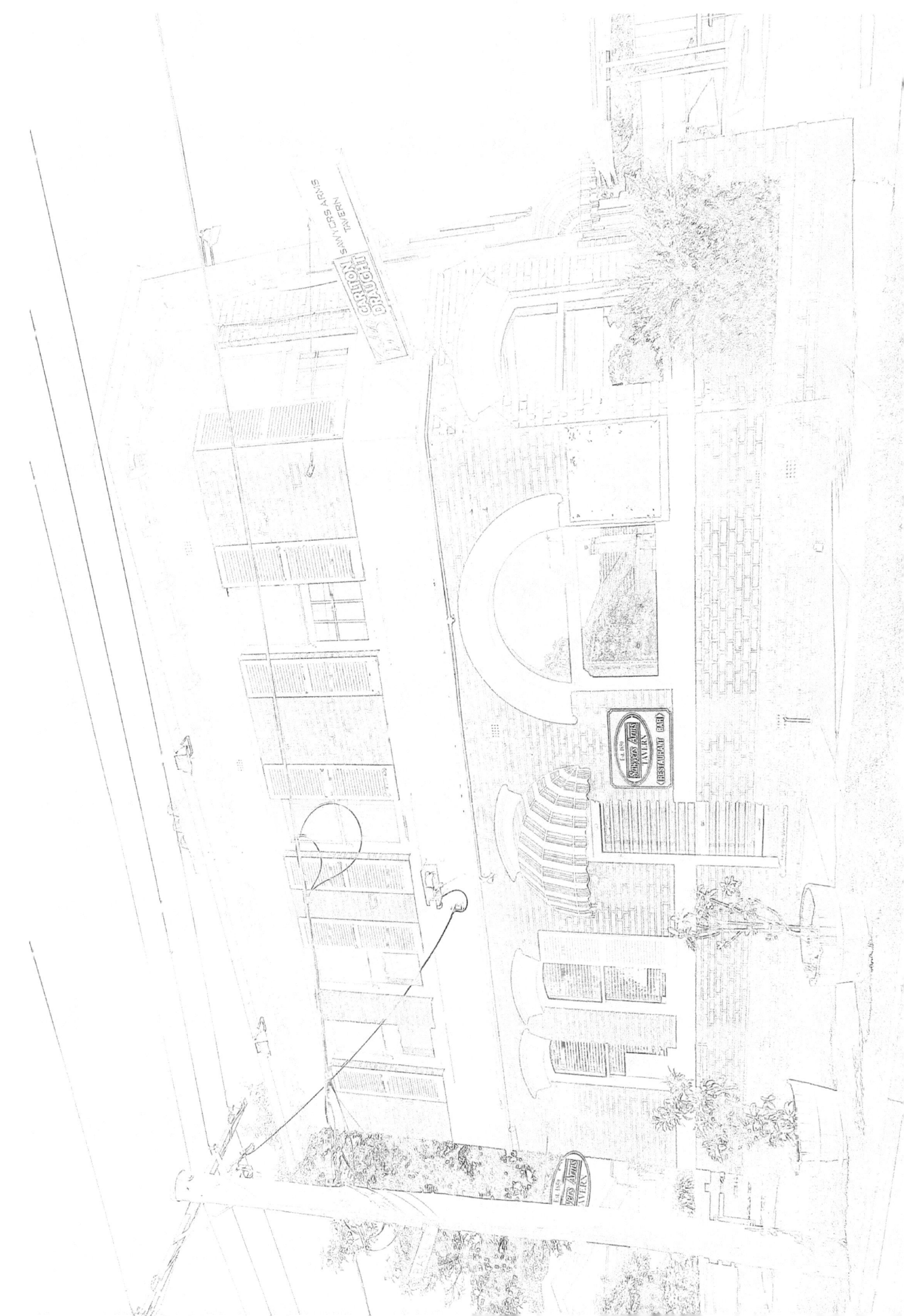

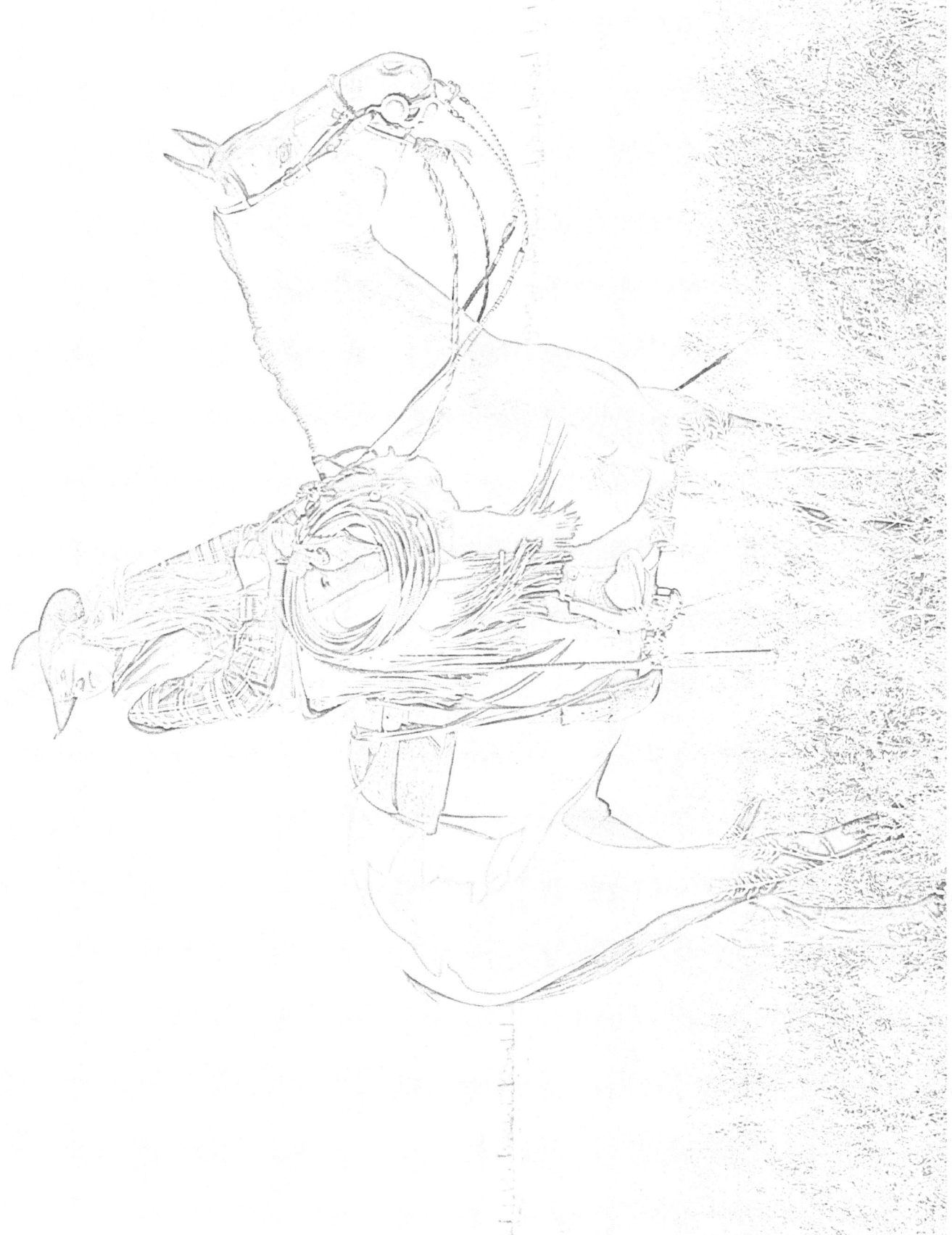

www.ingramcontent.com/pod-product-compliance
Lightning Source LLC
Chambersburg PA
CBHW081051180526
45170CB00005B/1760